A Smaller God

A Smaller God

*On the Divinely Human Nature
of Biblical Literature*

Petri Merenlahti
Foreword by David Rhoads

CASCADE *Books* • Eugene, Oregon

A SMALLER GOD

On the Divinely Human Nature of Biblical Literature

Copyright © 2015 Petri Merenlahti. All rights reserved. Except for brief quotations in critical publications or reviews, no part of this book may be reproduced in any manner without prior written permission from the publisher. Write: Permissions, Wipf and Stock Publishers, 199 W. 8th Ave., Suite 3, Eugene, OR 97401.

Cascade Books
An Imprint of Wipf and Stock Publishers
199 W. 8th Ave., Suite 3
Eugene, OR 97401

www.wipfandstock.com

All biblical quotations are from the New Revised Standard Version of the Bible, copyright © 1989 by the Division of Christian Education of the National Council of the Churches of Christ in the United States of America. Used with permission. All rights reserved.

ISBN 13: 978-1-62564-410-7

Cataloging-in-Publication data:

Merenlahti, Petri.

    A smaller God : on the divinely human nature of biblical literature / Petri Merenlahti.

    xiv + 120 p. ; 23 cm. — Includes bibliographical references and index.

    ISBN 13: 978-1-62564-410-7

    1. Bible—Criticism, interpretation, etc. 2. Bible—Psychology. I. Title.

BS600.3 .M327 2015

Manufactured in the U.S.A.

Truly I tell you, whoever does not receive the kingdom of God as a little child will never enter it (Mark 10:15).

When I was a child, I spoke like a child, I thought like a child, I reasoned like a child; when I became an adult, I put an end to childish ways (1 Cor 13:11).

Table of Contents

Foreword by David Rhoads ix

Preface xiii

1 A Divinely Human Book 1

2 A True Story? 12

3 An Immigrant God 31

4 So Much Out of So Little 48

5 A Malady or a Cure? 66

6 A Story without a Beginning 84

7 Childish Ways 99

Bibliography 107

Name and Subject Index 113

Scripture Index 117

Foreword

I love this book. And I plan to recommend it to friends and students. This is an honest book about religion and about the Bible. It is a vision of how to take the Bible as a source of truth, wisdom, and transformation without making an idol of it and without covering up its deep and profound flaws.

So if you are a person who takes the Bible literally and with a sense of absoluteness, this book by Petri Merenlahti will challenge you to see how others who think of the Bible as a collection of human writings nevertheless also experience its divine power to transform.

If you are someone who has rejected the Bible because others pushed it on you or allowed no questioning or shoved it down your throat, this book will be a breath of fresh air that may lead you to reconsider your disregard for the Bible.

And even if you have always thought of the Bible as a collection of literature written by humans but do not quite know why, then this book will no doubt help to clarify your thinking.

The book opens with a larger discussion of religion itself—the naked truth about the ways in which religion has led to the most horrifying evils, and how it has also been a transformative source of human compassion and goodness.

Religion has often been described as an opiate of the people, a source of self-deception, and an expression of mental disorder. Despite that, Petri insists that religion matters and that it is not going away. Religion cannot be reduced to psychology or science or anthropological studies. In its own right, religion plays an indispensable role in human life and society. So if religion in itself is not the problem, how can we view religion in such a way that it embraces a humane God and creates responsible human beings?

FOREWORD

Petri is especially concerned to counter the ways in which people take religious doctrine and the Bible as absolutes. Many of those who take this point of view consider the words of the Bible to be literal, absolute, universal, timeless truths about God and God's will for people. He is talking about what I might call "verbal idolatry"—every bit as dangerous as worshipping idols made of stone or of money.

Such a point of view can lead individuals and groups to assume an arrogant superiority that gives them the right to discriminate, suppress, and exercise violence against others who do not believe as they do. Christian history is filled with examples of groups that have used the Bible as justification for inquisitions, torture, slavery, suppression of women, exploitation of the poor, ethnic cleansing, witch hunts, holocausts of Jews, oppression of blacks, and discrimination against gays and lesbians.

Petri wants to articulate an alternative way to read the Bible. So in this book he examines the Bible as a human book that contains many problematic texts and statements of error, but which nevertheless, in other ways, can be a source of astounding goodness—a "divinely human" book as the subtitle suggests.

The critical question he poses at the end of the introduction is this: *What does it mean to say that the Bible is human?* The remainder of the book is comprised of five chapters that lay out how the Bible can and should be seen as a human book. The reflections are based on seeing the Bible as a collection of literature comprised of stories, wisdom, ethical reflection, and hymns of worship. Petri is looking here at how God and humans are portrayed in this human literature and what modern readers can make of it.

Petri observes that the choice between "fact or fiction" is a false choice. Clearly some biblical works, such as Jonah and Job, were meant to be fiction, even in ancient times. And historical writings are laced with fiction because the ancients told stories freely so as to bring out the "truth" about God and people rather than to be factually correct. So the human literature of the Bible has much to teach us and show us.

Petri emphasizes that the literature of the Bible comes from a very different culture and society in antiquity. I once heard Krister Stendahl say, "Reading Paul's letters is like reading someone else's mail." Indeed, this is true for all the writings of the Bible. We are "overhearing" stories and sayings that are addressed not directly to us but to those of a very different time and place. We should never assume that what *we* in our time make of those writing is what *they* understood them to mean.

FOREWORD

Because the authors of the Bible came from another society and culture, they assumed much that their ancient readers would understand. So for us, there are gaps to be filled and words to be understood in other ways than we might take them. We have to fill these gaps and assumptions with knowledge of biblical times—for example, honor-shame cultures, a limited-goods economy, religion embedded in politics, strict gender roles, and a society ordered according to "purity" and "defilement." Petri shows how this knowledge illuminates the stories in their time.

Yet once we have a handle on what a text may have meant, we still have to determine what implications it may or may not have for us in our time, what it means for us. This requires humility and the courage to make choices. Yet that is just what the Bible itself encourages human beings to do as we take responsibility for our lives in our circumstances today.

Perhaps most of all in this regard, Petri considers the Bible to be coming-of-age stories—both about God and about human characters. He sees the God who is a literary character in the Bible as one whose depiction changes and matures in fits and starts throughout the Hebrew Bible and the New Testament, from violence toward peace, from revenge toward mercy, from narrow loyalties toward an embrace of all. The Bible tells a story in which God gradually ceases to speak and appear externally until God disappears into the flesh of Jesus and ultimately becomes limitlessly present everywhere in and for all people.

At the same time, the Bible portrays a coming-of-age story for humans, a story in which God seeks to free humans from dependence upon God in unhealthy ways so that they take responsibility for their own decisions about what the Bible means and what God's will is today—so that, as Paul says, you might "Work out your own salvation in fear and trembling, for it is God who is at work in you" (Phil 2:12–13).

So for *us* to participate in this coming-of-age story, reading the Bible as a human book is in Petri's view to grow up—to see the Bible as it is, to wrestle with it, and to make hard choices to be faithful to it. We are called to "sin boldly"—that is, to take courageous actions without the certainty of correctness, without the fear of being wrong, and by letting humility and reverence for others guide the way.

If you love stories, you will relish this book. Petri obviously loves to tell stories, especially stories from the Bible about Ezekiel, David, Jonah, Job, Jesus, and Paul, but also other Jewish stories, personal stories, and stories from popular culture such as films. And he retells them in engaging ways, with insight and delight. These stories draw us into the biblical struggle between being realistic about life and at the same time embracing a vision of goodness to live for.

In this foreword, I have chosen to refer to the author of this book by his first name, Petri, because I have known him for many years, first as a visiting student from Finland, then as a fellow scholar, and now as a mentor who has helped me to see important nuances of biblical studies that had escaped me. This book reveals him as I have known him to be—a fine human being who is committed to manifesting the best of what humanity can become. I commend it to you.

David Rhoads
Emeritus Professor of New Testament
Lutheran School of Theology at Chicago

Preface

The story of this book began, so I have been told, on the Finnish national radio. Leena Majander, who was at the time the publishing director at Otava Publishing Company, was listening to *Who Is Who in World Literature*, a weekly series by the award-winning radio journalist Eeva Luotonen. Eeva was currently at the major characters of the Bible, and I had become a regular guest on her program. It seems that Leena liked what she heard, because she called the then editorial director, Tero Norkola, and asked him to persuade me to write a popular book about biblical literature and its interpretation.

I was delighted to take on the task—and, once the book came out, thrilled by its positive reception (it was short-listed for the Christian Book of the Year in Finland in 2007). During the next few years, I toyed with the idea of an English version, but it was only the insistence of my English language coach, Matt Cobb, that eventually gave me the courage to give it a try. I will always remain grateful to him for that. My sincere thanks go to Wipf & Stock for accepting the manuscript for publication. Also, I am in great debt to my senior colleagues, J. Harold Ellens, Halvor Moxnes, Heikki Räisänen, David Rhoads, Wayne Rollins, and Kari Syreeni for their encouragement and support.

What I needed then was time and money for writing. These became available when another colleague of mine, Elina Vuola, became professor of the Finnish Academy in 2013. She was kind enough to invite me to her research team and let me include this book in my work plan. When the director of Finn Church Aid, Antti Pentikäinen, generously granted me leave from my position there, I was all set for the work.

PREFACE

Now that work is done. While the bulk of the present book follows the original Finnish version, some parts are quite new. I have rewritten the first and the last chapters, so as to sharpen my thesis and consider some recent debates on the goods and evils of religion. On the other hand, I have also made use of some of my previous publications. The opening pages of Chapter 2 were originally included in "Reading as a Little Child: On the Model Reader of the Gospels" in the Oxford University Press Journal *Literature and Theology*, vol. 18, no. 2 (2004) 139–52. Chapters 2, 4, 5, and 7 contain portions of a piece, "Distorted Reality or Transitional Space? Biblical Miracle Stories in Psychoanalytic Perspective," that I wrote for the collection *Miracles: God, Science, and Psychology in the Paranormal, Vol I: Religious and Spiritual Events*, edited by J. Harold Ellens, 15–35 (Westport, CT: Praeger, 2008). Chapters 4 and 6 contain a few lines from my previous book, *Poetics for the Gospels? Rethinking Narrative Criticism* (New York: T & T Clark, 2002). Chapter 5 contains parts of an article, "So Who Really Needs Therapy? On Psychological Exegesis and Its Subject," in *Svensk Exegetisk Årsbok* (*Swedish Exegetical Yearbook*) 72 (2007) 7–30.

Both life and publishing are teamwork, and I have been fortunate to have the best of teams. I wish to thank the editorial team at Wipf and Stock, Christian Amondson, Heather Carraher, Rodney Clapp, Laura Poncy, and Matthew Wimer, for their helpfulness, great commitment, and high-quality professionalism. And I wish to thank my dear home team, Anu, Lahja, Saimi, and Vilho, for being there for me and sharing my joys and sorrows of writing.

Finally, in terms of language, one thing needs to be mentioned. Finnish is gender neutral by nature. There are no separate pronouns for male and female. So, writing in English, I encountered a problem I originally did not have: how to refer to the biblical God. Eventually, I decided for the masculine pronoun, not because I think God is male, but to convey the historical androcentricism of biblical times and the aura of masculinity that surrounds the character of God in biblical literature. Again, I want to emphasize that in my mind, this, too, is part of the contingent, human nature of the Bible. I would not conceive of a gendered God.

1

A Divinely Human Book

Religion Returns

In today's world, religion divides people like a sword. The spectrum of opinions is wide and rich with extremes. For some, faith remains an unparalleled pathway to a purposeful life. Others regard it as simply wicked, nothing short of a cancer of the human race. In between, there are a growing number of people who remain resolutely indifferent towards any organized religion, either because they insist on a personalized kind of spirituality of their own, or because religion simply isn't their type of a thing at all.

Typically, each of these groups thinks the others have misunderstood religion completely. When militant atheists, for example, claim that religious beliefs are unreasonable, apologists say this is not the faith they know of. In their view, God must be transcendent; otherwise, any talk of God would make no sense at all. This is to say that claims about God are of a different order than claims about the ordinary things of our everyday world. Therefore, it makes a poor argument to say that religion is irrational on the grounds that there is as little evidence of God as there is of, say, Bertrand Russell's proverbial teapot orbiting the earth. That would be comparing apples and oranges.

The atheists, on the other hand, would advise us to take a good look at what average religious people are really like. A thoroughly transcendent God may well suit philosophers and theologians, but ordinary believers are in it for real. They are not spending their days contemplating some ethereal moral principle. Rather, they keep vivid and personal relations with a hilariously motley crew of gods, saints, spirits, and angels they think are quite present and perfectly real. To deny that would go against facts, and to call it primitive, superstitious, or otherwise inauthentic as religion would only show condescension.

Lastly, the great majority of people seem unlikely to join either the theologically sophisticated or the blatantly atheist camp. By all accounts, religion is not going away. Unlike what was predicted by many social scientists just a couple of decades ago, modern life, a higher standard of living, and better education did not make faith redundant. On the contrary, by the end of the last millennium religion had returned with a vengeance, and the form in which it reappeared was not contemplative or philosophically intricate but, in a variety of proportions, charismatic, consumerist, and political. Christian Pentecostalism swept over sub-Saharan Africa and Latin America, combining intense emotion with a straightforward prosperity gospel. In Europe, glossy magazines showcased do-it-yourself kits of spiritual healing, yoga exercise, and coffee-table Buddhism to their worldly cosmopolitan readers. The Christian religious right, Hindu and Buddhist nationalism, and radical Islam reintroduced religion to politics in their respective constituencies. Amidst it all, an even greater number of people who may feel positive about their religion, or remain happily indifferent to any, all agree that bigotry, pious or secular, is plainly annoying. Mainstream and extremism do not attract each other—that is, after all, why they are called mainstream and extremism.

The Dark Side of Religion

Yet religion matters, and there is something to it that remains unlike anything else. When the critics and champions of faith point out its evils and blessings, respectively, they are not making those up. Horrible atrocities take place, not just in the name of religion but due to the fervor it incites in pious minds: terrorist attacks, ethnic cleansing, persecution of minorities, mass murder, collective suicide, holy war. On the other hand, religions also encourage people to suppress their ego and search for the common good; they advocate the cause of the poor and inspire campaigns for social justice; and, sometimes, they inspire extraordinary deeds that can only be described as saintly or heroic. More than half of all education and health care services in sub-Saharan Africa are currently provided by faith-based organizations, to pick just one example.

How can such an odd combination be? How should a commitment to the finest of ideals accord with extreme evil? Is there a particular demon for religious people, something they should come to recognize, so as to be able to fight it? This question is as old as religion itself.

It is tempting to cut the question short and conclude that religion itself is the problem. After all, what did you expect? Primitive systems of belief are hardly a match to modern empirical thinking, are they?

Yet religious faith and a modern, scientific understanding of the world need not be mutually exclusive. Quite many people seem happy to embrace both. It is true that the devil is in the details and if pressed hard, many such people might lack the conceptual tools to explain how exactly the two modes of experience go together. But the point is that they do not feel the need to press that hard, as long as it all works out in rough figures. If you want to know how the universe came into being and how it works, go ask a scientist; if you're interested in the meaning of life and wonder how you should live, turn to religion. Some corners of the United States apart, serious creationism remains a marginal phenomenon, and it is not unusual even for an Islamist activist in Europe to hold a Western university degree in science or technology.

Nor need holding on to a religious conviction mean that you replace your independent moral judgment for some archaic piece of ancient law. On the contrary, most religious authorities would suggest that you put that moral judgment into frequent use. Roman Catholicism and Lutheranism, for example, are major Christian denominations, and their adherents are taught that in moral terms Christians are in no way different from any other people. They all should consult their natural, God-given sense of morality. Therefore, as Luther put it, an irreligious sage makes a better ruler than a pious fool. What to do with the regrettable limitations all men and women have in duly following their moral senses, and the wish to be absolved from that, is a different matter entirely.

In fact, the core moral and spiritual teachings of major world religions are hardly unusual or outdated. On the contrary, many of them make perfect and universal sense: life is precious and rich with meaning; there is hope for humanity and the world; love your neighbor as yourself.

So, are holy wars and religious violence actually about something else than faith altogether? Is their true root cause not religion at all, but human prejudice, envy, greed, or hunger for power? After all, religions don't kill people, people do. This, too, can be an attractive thought. Yet as Katherine Marshall, senior fellow at the Berkley Centre for Religion, Peace, and World Affairs at Georgetown University, puts it, "religion is not cuddly" but raw and passionate and therefore at perpetual risk of going awry.

With religion, stakes are always high. In a fine study, *When Religion Becomes Evil: Five Warning Signs*, the Baptist minister and professor of religion Charles Kimball lists several features that make religion prone to abuse: religions make absolute truth claims and promote universal values; they require discipline and obedience; they foster utopian visions of a world more worthy that the one we currently live in; they feel strongly for what they regard as holy; and they are not afraid to stand up for what they think is right. While none of this is detrimental as such, there is no limit to the damage that will follow if any of these principles are taken to extremes. When that occurs, the link between religion and violence is not accidental. Rather, it will result in a specific kind of abuse that is religious in nature. It comes in all sizes and colors. People's thoughts and behavior may be controlled minutely by a totalitarian authority. An assertive spiritual leader may impose a rule of blind obedience over his or her flock. The quest for doctrinal or ritual purity may lead to discrimination against minorities, or it may ignite utopian frenzy, so that those caught in it try to force an apocalypse.

Ideals and Reality

Religion is all about ideals that are larger than life and beyond the reach of mortal men. Therein lie its risks and its strengths. Religion makes it possible to postulate such hard-to-find things as the highest good, the right way to live, eternal values, enduring hope, and selfless love. Access to such ideals, provided by religion or some other life-stance, is likely to be essential to human well-being. Once removed, cynicism, bitterness, and disillusionment will be quick to take their place.

Yet people can become addicted to their ideals, so that the mere thought of them being flawed becomes unbearable for them.

In reality, no religion is the perfect mother: it cannot meet anyone's every single need or demand. This is hardly the purpose of religion (or the purpose of mothering, as the British psychoanalyst D.W. Winnicott did so well to point out), either. Like all human experience, spiritual life, too, is bound to involve frustration. Lest this disturb the ideal image, frustration may then become repressed from the conscious mind—only to return as personal guilt ("what a bad Christian am I to think like this") or outright paranoia ("this is all about our enemies wanting to destroy us"). Such thinking is typical of religious extremists, and it reveals how reliant they are on absolute good and unconditional recognition. In an extremist framework, good and bad cannot coexist; imperfection will inevitably destroy the good and turn it into evil. This is why extremists must keep their ideals (or better, their idealized images of things that were never meant to be ideal in the first place) unpolluted. To contain imperfection, they need an equally airtight depository of what is bad: a community of enemies—"children of darkness"—whose wicked character is beyond any reasonable doubt.

All religions must grapple the question of balance between divine ideals and human imperfection. This may well be the very purpose of religion; as the Canadian literary critic Patrick Grant says, religions spell out the human predicament of being "confronted by the scandal of suffering and imperfection while aspiring nonetheless to ideals marked by the absence of such things." To be human is to embrace ideals that are both nonnegotiable and unattainable. Moreover, it is imperative that they remain so, lest our ideals become delusions. In Grant's words, "aspirations to perfection should awaken us to our actual imperfection."[1] No wonder, then, that reflections of this very dilemma are so deeply embedded in the religious traditions of the world. One holy writ after another underlines that no human entity, be it a text, a teaching, or a spiritual leader, must ever be assigned a sovereignly divine status. Similarly, being part of a holy community has no value in itself. It becomes meaningless if the community neglects the demands of love and justice. Ancient teachings that insist on this point abound, and they are meant to curb false idealization and the ego inflation that follows in its wake.

Nevertheless, holy texts themselves are frequently idealized. Fundamentalist movements are adamant about scriptural inerrancy. Disputes between progressive and conservative Christians typically boil down to the question of biblical authority. If the Holy Bible was written by mortal men (as all Christians admit it was; the debates about the Holy Quran will be trickier from the start), how can it be God's word? If it is God's word, what to think of its dark side, that is, teachings that are clearly against common morality? After all, in addition to the doctrine of neighborly love, the Bible

---

1. Grant, *Imperfection*, 4–5.

also contains instructions for a holy war. The orders are to spare no one, civilians and domestic animals included.

As Protestant Christians in particular will know, sacred writings make immense authority accessible to anyone. In Shakespeare's words, even the devil can cite Scripture for his purpose. So do human religious and political leaders, and a random quote from Scripture remains good currency in many quarters. The Bible and the Quran have been applied in support of sending men to slavery, women to the stake, and children to the minefields. There cannot be any serious doubt that mistaking human vision for divine judgment is fatally dangerous and should be avoided at all cost. This is, also, why the question, "What exactly does it mean that the Bible is human literature?" is a very practical one, and massively acute at that.

There Is No Such Thing as Biblical Literalism

Christians are fortunate to have the kind of Scriptures you literally cannot take by the letter. No original manuscript of the Old or New Testament has survived, nor are the ones we have completely identical. Different editions, as well as the translations based on them, all rely on some scholarly compromise. While the differences are mostly minor, some of them are remarkable (a number of Christian churches, for example, came to adopt the larger collection of books included in the Greek Old Testament, while others preferred the shorter, so-called Masoretic version of the Hebrew Bible), and standard translations adapt to the latest version of their chosen critical edition of the Greek and Hebrew text, respectively.

For most Christians, none of this has ever been a major problem. Unlike the Jews and the Muslims, for whom only the Hebrew and Arabic texts, respectively, count as true Scripture, Christians have invested heavily in translation. The gospel was to be preached to all nations, so you made your translation the best you could out of the manuscripts you were fortunate to have. While some translations—like the Latin Vulgate, or the English King James Bible—came to enjoy great veneration, there was never any ecumenical decision on the exact wording of the Christian Bible.

Besides, even if you somehow did reach an agreement about the wording, it would still be quite difficult to follow your Bible literally on every single point—at least if a literalist reading should mean there was no interpretation involved. First, a great deal of what the Bible says is contextual. Sometimes it fits to beat your swords into plowshares (Isa 2:4, Mic 4:3) and sometimes the other way round (Joel 3:10). Second, not all biblical writers agreed even on the most important issues. While Paul held that "a person is justified by faith apart from works prescribed by the law" (Rom 3:28), James was confident that "faith apart from works is barren" (2:20) and "a person is justified by works and not by faith alone" (2:24). Third, as all understanding involves an amount of interpretation, most texts have not one but many "literal meanings." Translators in particular are well aware of this, as they wrestle endlessly with ambiguous expressions and alternative readings.

Moreover, meanings do change from one time and place to another. When Jesus says that the kingdom of God belongs to those who are like little children, what does he mean? The way childhood is understood, and what it is like to live as a child in any given surroundings, depend on culture and social class (among other things). This, too, is why different people come up with different "literal" readings of one and the same text.

The Human Nature of the Christian Bible

To think of God's word as incarnate in a mutable human form (of literature, or the man Jesus) is, of course, neither new nor alien to Christians. Rather, that is the climactic high point of the great Christian narrative: God puts aside his divine glory and assumes the limitations of human life, so that the infinite may make contact with the transient. When God speaks to human beings, he adjusts his message to their language, so as to suit their limited human experience. He becomes a smaller God, of human size.

It is therefore quite appropriate that narrative should be the central medium of the Christian message. Unlike doctrinal statements or legal statutes, narratives are oblique and ambiguous by nature. What one audience thinks is the turning point of the story may pass unnoticed by another. Also, there is always more to a narrative than its meaning. People read and listen to stories not only for education, but for pleasure and excitement. That is why narrative is so close to human nature, or better, the human soul. This is most tangible in the New Testament Gospels, which—as the early critics of Christianity never grew tired of pointing out—mostly represent a rather unrefined variety of popular literature. Yet what did they expect of a countercultural movement that featured ordinary peasants and fishermen as God's envoys, and quislings and prostitutes as his chosen people?

When people turn to religion, they often embark on a journey of recovery and personal growth: my life was a mess, I was grieved, the future seemed bleak, and then, suddenly (or sometimes gradually), all that changed. In moments like this, faith is not so much what it says in the catechism of your church; rather, it is a fresh story about God, who takes interest in human life and appears in such a form that fits in human circumstances. Ever since the dawn of Christianity, intellectuals have been wary of such a popular God, yet he has a steady appeal for those whose faith is less about philosophy and more about why to get up in the morning.

Christians soon realized how essential it was that their Lord and the good news they proclaimed had both divine authority and human appeal. The idea of the Christ's two natures, human and divine, became indispensable. Not all of its implications were always easy to pull through, though—especially so in issues related to the human body. Some church fathers, for example, insisted that the Christ had a special kind of digestive system that produced no excrement at all. According to St. John Chrysostom, Jesus never laughed. Apparently, undignified, uncontrolled bodily functions were not among the things you'd expect of your Savior, no matter how human he otherwise may have been.

It is of equally little surprise that modern biblical criticism should make some pious minds troubled. Isn't it simply improper to scrutinize Scripture like any other old piece of literature, independently of it being God's word? The results of biblical scholarship tend to create confusion, too: one can understand that Moses did not write the five books ascribed to him—after all, would he recount his own death in the past tense? (Deut 34)—but surely the Pauline letters must be of Pauline origin, if the Bible tells us so? On the other hand, some evangelists were quite open about their use of sources (Luke 1:1–4), nor did they expect their readers to think they were omniscient. In the Gospels, Jesus himself is sometimes taken by surprise.

Mainline churches did not reject modern scholarship. On the contrary, biblical criticism is now a sturdy part of the curriculum in countless seminaries, theological colleges, and divinity schools. This is to make sure that the human and the divine aspects of reality, the Jewish prophet Jesus and Jesus the Son of God, are seen as the two sides of the same coin. The divine history of salvation is inseparable from the human history of a tribal religion in the ancient Middle East.

So, it is not only that churches can no longer pretend critical scholarship wasn't there. Rather, mainstream Christianity insisted from early on that human knowledge and divine wisdom are compatible. From a Christian point of view, history was always both about a divine plan and about human pursuits. Jesus' God-given role as the divine Savior did not make his humanity ostensible. Instead, it made new sense of what God and humans are like.

A God with a Human Face?

Incarnate in a literary character, the biblical God develops and changes shape. He is bound to do so, as the biblical books are many and feature several different genres. The Jewish and Christian Scriptures were written over hundreds of years by different people, for different audiences, in different circumstances, and for different purposes. Therefore, the story about how the Bible came into being is at the same time a story about God's coming-of-age.

In the paradise story, God is still conspicuously humanlike. When he approaches in the cool of the evening, you can hear him coming by the sound of his footsteps in the garden. This early image of God is quite unlike the Almighty as he would later become known. This is a tribal God, one among many, jealous and impulsive. He is not fond of being cheated on (but has to suffer it, as the rulers of his chosen people are notoriously prone to worship foreign gods).

Toward younger parts of the Bible, the picture becomes different. Now it is not so much tribal loyalty as justice and compassion that God requires from those who call out his name. The God of Israel is transformed into a universal heavenly father who does not care if you are Jew or Greek, slave or free, male or female (Gal 3:28).

As the Pulitzer-winning author Jack Miles has pointed out (see his masterpieces, *God: A Biography*, and *Christ: A Crisis in the Life of God*), God ends up disarming himself. In his wild youth, he may well have given hell to Sodomites, Egyptians, and Amalekites. He was resolute then, and his hand did not waver; justice was done on the spot. As time went on, however, he grew more patient and more prone to postpone his verdict. Before long, all appeals came to be referred to an eschatological Last Judgment. Until that day, humans should see it for themselves. You reap whatever you sow: bad deeds will cost you the trust and respect of other people. At other times, virtue will be its own reward: you will become like your Father in heaven. In no case, however, can you tell God's approval from your present lot in this transient world. "He makes his sun rise on the evil and on the good, and sends rain on the righteous and on the unrighteous" (Matt 5:45).

The change in God's character goes together with an improved sense of reality. No more a superhero at the service of human fantasy, the matured God acts like a responsible parent. He helps his children tolerate the harsh facts of life, yet he insists that faith, hope, and love are still worth a try. As Miles sums up, God gradually finds out who he is and what it means to be God for humans.

The Human Side of the Bible: Five Aspects

To repeat the question, what exactly does it mean that the Bible is human by nature? The next five chapters lay out my attempt at an answer. I believe that if we dare to give up the idealized images we may have, the reward will be a healthy, balanced relationship with something real. Once we understand that biblical ideas about God did not descend from heaven but were discovered and, sometimes, reconsidered, in the course of history, it will be easier for us to be honest about them. Otherwise, there is the risk that we split away and repress the unpleasant parts, as if they are not there. And there is really no need for that. Imperfection will not turn all good things into bad. Whatever is valuable in the Bible will remain so, even if we admit that the Good Book is sometimes wide of the mark—as it indeed seems to be: today, there are no grounds to believe that the sun orbits the earth; that homosexual behavior is an abomination; or that women come second to men, even though a good number of biblical writers did think just that. Thanks to science and education, we now know better, and that makes us better readers of the Bible, too.

I suggest there are five aspects to what makes the Bible human and, therefore, imperfect. None of them, I think, make biblical literature any more (or less) senseless or immoral than the rest of the human culture on average. Rather, it is the very sincere biblical aspirations to perfection that make biblical imperfections stand out in the first place. In this respect, the Bible is all but a most typical collection of sacred texts.

So, what are those five aspects of biblical imperfection? First, the biblical narrative is neither the unedited truth nor pure invention. Instead, the different books of the Bible employ a number of literary registers, from ancient history writing to comic pastiche. It is the very peculiar combination of history, myth, tradition, and fiction that makes the Bible simultaneously contextual and timeless.

Second, the Bible originates in a particular, foreign culture. People in ancient Mediterranean culture felt, thought, and acted differently, so that we may often fail to understand what they meant to say or do. Cultural mobility and conflict are in the very nature of biblical literature. The history of the Scriptures, their creation, contents, and reception, are all about leaving home, becoming a refugee, and living in a foreign land. The biblical God is a refugee himself, forever in the process of integration.

Third, biblical characters—including God—are literary. Even when based on real life, they are products of artistic design. As such, they have a number of salient characteristics peculiar to biblical literature. Sometimes those characteristics carry special meaning, so that certain literary features become constitutive of what the Bible has to say about humanity. Biblical anthropology assumes the form of storytelling.

Fourth, there are psychological patterns to how people understand and relate to God in the Bible. These can be complex, and they evolve through time. Some of them are intentional, while others remain unconscious, and they can give birth to fantasies as well as nightmares. Therefore, some biblical texts are inspirational and others full of anxiety.

Finally, all our readings depend on interpretation—and our interpretations, in turn, depend on the place, time, and culture we happen to live in. This is why the Bible needs to be constantly interpreted anew. The process of reinterpretation started in the Bible itself, as many biblical authors and editors commented on and revised the work of their predecessors. Later, such creative rereading became the means for churches and synagogues to keep their Scriptures in tune with the times. This required that they be imaginative, adaptive, and tolerant—all fine qualities and still in great demand.

So, where will these five steps take us? To some limp, diluted version of the Christian religion, disenchanted and demythologized? I think not. Rather, they will guide our way past what is secondary, irrelevant, or outright harmful, to the very essence of faith. Our reward will be wisdom instead of fanaticism, peace instead of guilt and hatred, and compassion instead of merciless moralism. We will learn that whoever wants to be holy must be kind, as Jesus is kind: while he urges his followers to imitate God and strive for perfection, he is unafraid of being polluted by their actual shortcomings. Instead, he purifies everything he reaches out to touch. He is human. He is not inhumane.

2

A True Story?

Fact or Fiction?

A few days before a Christmas past I was reading a bedtime story to my then-three-year-old daughter. It was called "Dandelion" and it was written by the Finnish author Leena Erkkilä. It began like this (the translation is mine):

> In those times when our heavenly father was making trees and forests and flowers and weeds, something like this might well have happened.[1]

At this point my daughter interrupted me and asked: "Who is this heavenly father?"

In spite of all my theological education, I blinked. Impatient, she snapped, "All right, the story just has him there," and urged me to carry on. Which I did, and then we read a couple of other stories about certain carrots and rubber balls, and the question was left aside.

What went on there in the little girl's mind during that short moment of silence? I think it went like this: she pondered the situation and concluded that, apparently, no extrinsic knowledge was necessary. Whatever she might need to know either would be available in the narrative itself or could be inferred from what she already knew about stories. So, she would

---

1. Erkkilä, *Kukkutimurusia*, 5.

think, let us assume a heavenly father who, by definition, is responsible for the existence of vegetation on earth, and, then, let us hear what sort of things the story has to say about him.

What is striking, from an adult point of view, is the remarkable openness that a child reader can grant a narrative, that is, how huge the gaps in the story are that can be left for her imagination to fill in. She really is the maker of the story she hears. Yet the principle is the same in the case of adult readers, too. They take it as a fact that stories are somewhat smaller worlds than the one we live in and that we must make them complete as we read by supplying some necessary extra information. To use the example once given by the Italian author and critic Umberto Eco: if a historical novel that takes place in nineteenth-century France tells of people who are traveling in a carriage, it need not mention that the carriage was pulled by a horse.

If necessary, the readers will also accept that story worlds can be imaginary or fictional and, for this reason, quite different from the world we live in—that "something like this might well have happened" but probably did not. If the story includes speaking wolves, the readers won't let that bother them. This is because the moment the readers started reading the narrative they made an agreement, as it were, with the storyteller, which licensed a game of make-believe, just like children make in their own games of a similar type: "Let's pretend she is invisible and you can't see her." "Let's pretend there's a heavenly father who once made all the trees and the flowers." "The story just has him there."

In practice, my daughter's hypothesis worked out fine. She could listen to the story and afterwards there was no need to return to the question concerning the factual identity of our heavenly father.

But was her hypothesis correct? Did she read the story as the storyteller expected her to read it? I think not. I think the words "the story just has him there" implied that our heavenly father belonged to the same category of characters as gnomes, elves, and Winnie the Pooh—that is, that the story at this point made no reference to any real person outside the story.

Now I do know people who do not think God and Winnie the Pooh are that different. As they see it, God, too, is a kind of fiction that enables us to deal with the meaning of life and that sort of thing. Yet I do think that these people, too, would consider our heavenly father an "immigrant character" (Terence Parsons's term) in a fictional bedtime story.[2] Whatever you think religion is, it is something other than a game of make-believe

---

2. See Parsons, *Nonexistent Objects*.

("Let's pretend there's a God and we believe in him."). Rather, God is serious business. Even an imagined God, although designed just for the purposes of literary art, is prone to break the limits of the narrative and enter into reality where matters are given serious consideration. A possible world becomes a possible credo. What if God was like this? What were we supposed to think then? And indeed, wherever these possible credos become considered a threat, the faithful take to the streets, indices are made, and books are burned. Even a *fatwa* may be issued to haunt some unfortunate fantasist like the Indian author Salman Rushdie.

Yet in principle, the line between fact and fiction is clear enough—at least most of the time. Around Christmas, we sat together and listened to the second chapter of Luke's gospel, my daughter and I. I could see it in her eyes that she was thinking hard, and after a moment she asked me: "Dad, when will we go and meet this little baby Jesus?"

Once upon a Time There Was a Prophet

Unlike bedtime stories, the New Testament Gospels are not fiction. When an evangelist says that in those days there was a certain ruler in Syria or a young couple in Galilee, he means just that. Whether it actually was so in those days, is a different matter—some readers are convinced and others are not. Yet the "once upon a time" of a fairy tale and the "once upon a time" of the Bible are two different things. The former is the narrator's invitation to a game of make-believe. The latter asks to be taken at face value, as an account of holy history or sacred tradition.

There are exceptions, though, and these need to be mentioned. An important one is the book of Jonah, a surrealistic comedy about a wayward rebel of a prophet who resents God's leniency. His name, Jonah, stands for a dove, and the dove is one of the symbols of God's chosen people. This provides us with the first clue that what we are about to hear is a satire about religious complacency.

The story begins like any other prophetic book:

> Now the word of the Lord came to Jonah son of Amittai, saying, "Go at once to Nineveh, that great city, and cry out against it; for their wickedness has come up before me." (Jonah 1:1–2)

What follows then, however, is something completely different. God tells Jonah to go east, yet the obstinate prophet embarks on a ship he hopes

A TRUE STORY?

will take him as far west as he can get, away from the presence of the Lord. The diversion does not quite work, and the Lord hurls an impressive gale upon the sea. While the mariners cry out, each to his own god, and throw the cargo into the sea, Jonah is fast asleep in the hold of the ship. The crew casts lots to find out who is to blame for the calamity, and the lot falls on Jonah. Upon asking who he is and where he comes from, Jonah boasts to be a Hebrew and a servant of the Lord, creator of the universe (being absent without leave apparently isn't a reason for Jonah not to take credit for his piety). The heathen sailors are terrified; unlike Jonah, they show some proper fear of God. Jonah advises them to throw him into the sea to calm down the storm. After trying in vain to row the ship back to land, and apologizing to God in case Jonah should be innocent after all, they throw him overboard. The sea calms down at once. God sends a giant fish to swallow up Jonah, and Jonah spends three days in its belly. Biding his time, he sings a beautiful psalm to the Lord, after which the Lord orders the fish to spew Jonah out on dry land: end of act one.

Back at square one, God gives it another try:

> The word of the Lord came to Jonah a second time, saying, "Get up, go to Nineveh, that great city, and proclaim to it the message that I tell you." So Jonah set out and went to Nineveh, according to the word of the Lord. (Jonah 3:1–3)

Nineveh was no small city, but in this story it is absolutely huge, "a three days' walk across." Jonah makes his sermon short: "Forty days more, and Nineveh shall be overthrown!" Yet his words turn out to be extremely effective: everyone believes and repents. The king proclaims a general hunger strike—no one is to taste any food or drink—and even animals are covered with sackcloth, in the hope that God might relent and save the city.

And of course he does. Moved by the people's anguish, God has mercy on them. This is more than Jonah can take. What? No fire and brimstone? All that hard work for nothing, and now he must look like a complete idiot! "I knew it," he protests to God, "I told you so! This is precisely why I did not want to go in the first place. You never had any intention to do anything to these people, did you? Why don't you just kill me? I mean, please, save me from the embarrassment." After this outburst, Jonah marches out of the city gates, sits in the scorching sun, and casts an occasional hopeful glance at the city: perhaps it might end up badly after all?

Meanwhile, God has a bush grow up over Jonah, to give shade over his head. Jonah is pleased, but the next morning, a worm chews up the bush, so that it withers. The sultry east wind blows, the sun beats down on Jonah's head, and Jonah wishes he was dead. God is puzzled:

> You are concerned about the bush, for which you did not labor and which you did not grow; it came into being in a night and perished in a night. And should I not be concerned about Nineveh, that great city, in which there are more than a hundred and twenty thousand persons who do not know their right hand from their left, and also many animals? (Jonah 4:10–11)

The book of Jonah is a mischievous parody of a prophet's plight and his petty martyrdom. It makes appropriate fun of the idea that the Almighty God should want to serve the vain interests of a self-righteous elite; or that he, the compassionate creator of the universe, would ever think of his creations as a dull mass. As the story goes on, the heathen Ninevites prove to be more God-fearing than the Hebrew prophet, and the Lord refuses to discipline them no matter how bad that should make Jonah look. Finally, God's concluding words turn the biblical idea of holy war upside down. In a holy war, as it was prescribed in earlier biblical tradition, you were supposed to kill everyone, animals included. In the book of Jonah, not only has God mercy on a foreign nation. He is also concerned that their many animals should not be harmed.

A Human Tragedy

The character of Jonah is a living proof that the Bible can make fun of itself by means of satiric fiction: a prophet might well have looked like this.

Besides Jonah, there is yet another biblical book that presents radical ideas in the form of literary fiction. The book of Job is a tragic poem about a question that was as topical at the time as it is now: why do bad things happen to good people? The answer: God is not just in the conventional, human sense of the word. Life is not fair, innocent people suffer, and evildoers go unpunished.

In the opening scene, God boasts to Satan about Job, that man of exceptional virtue he is proud to have as his servant. Satan is unsurprisingly cynical: untried, Job's good behavior is as good as nothing. Test him, and he will fail:

> Does Job fear God for nothing? Have you not put a fence around him and his house and all that he has, on every side? You have

blessed the work of his hands, and his possessions have increased in the land. But stretch out your hand now, and touch all that he has, and he will curse you to your face. (Job 1:9–11)

God accepts the challenge, and Satan is allowed a free ride with Job. Job loses his property, family, and health, yet he will not curse God.

At this point, Job's three friends, Eliphaz the Temanite, Bildad the Shuhite, and Zophar the Naamathite, hear about his misfortune and come to offer him consolation. They sit together in silence for a week. Then Job opens his mouth and lets it all out. His speech marks the end of the introductory narrative. What follows is the actual poetic work, a dialogue between Job and his friends. In due time, it is joined first by a young man, Elihu the Buzite, and then by God himself.

Job's point is that God has wronged him. Whatever he is being punished for, he did not do it.

Job's friends will not agree with him. God is almighty and just, they say, and this is why the righteous will prosper while the godless perish. So, there must be something Job has done to deserve his present distress. Job rejects this, but admits there is little he can do. Though the heavens fall, you cannot press charges against God.

For once, however, God does show up for the hearing. In the two concluding speeches of the play, God answers Job—albeit the answer comes in the form of a series of questions: "I will question you, and you shall declare to me" (Job 38:3).

God wants to know if Job thinks God is the kind of creature humans can truly grasp. He thus puts Job back in his proper place. Yet at the same time, God vindicates Job and reproaches his friends: Job certainly did not deserve his sufferings. While God does rule over everything, his ways are far beyond human comprehension. Therefore, being unfortunate is no sign of being godless.

Job replies by pulling back his charges against God. He understands that God's purposes are unknowable to humans, so that whatever life brings, you should not take it personally. Suffering is not about divine punishment, it is about being human, that is, imperfect, vulnerable, fragile.

Like the book of Jonah, the book of Job, too, is a theological fiction. This time, comedy gives way to tragedy. Together with Job and his friends, we learn a lesson about the human condition.

Is it pure coincidence that the two literary fictions, Jonah and Job, should also be the most humanistic pieces of literature in the Holy Bible?

Artistic freedom goes well together with a vision of religious tolerance. Once people are granted the right to stage an imaginary debate with God, they must also be free to question any given canon, doctrine, or creed in the light of their personal experience.

The Gospel Truth

In the case of Jonah and Job, it is relatively easy to explain—even to a three-year-old—what kind of stories they are and whether they are true or not. Both books are fiction, yet they do have something important to say: while God is not always cuddly, he nonetheless loves his creatures, and the hardships life makes them endure are not signs of his anger.

What about the rest of the Bible, then? Are the other biblical books in it for real? At this point, things become complicated.

Many biblical figures and events are historical. Critical scholarship is virtually unanimous that Jesus, a Jewish prophet and popular healer from Galilee, really did exist. So did Paul, the man who devoted his life to making the community of Jesus' disciples global; a number of his authentic writings have survived. Kings of Israel and Judah appear in historical sources outside the Bible as well.

That said, it is only very little that we know about them. The biblical authors preferred to keep their characterization scarce. Nor were they interested in history as such; what mattered was how it revealed and confirmed a divine plan.

So, when the Hebrew Bible recounts the history of the kingdoms of Judah and Israel, the aim is to show that their downfall was not due to the weakness of their patron god, the Lord. Instead, it was a due punishment for the transgressions of their rulers. They broke their covenant with the Lord by worshipping foreign gods. Once the people return to their true God, a new, blessed era of happiness will begin.

The New Testament builds upon a similar master narrative: even though Jesus ended up being tortured to death, this was not a failure after all. It was rather a most honorable act of courage, a vicarious sacrifice for many, authorized and predestined by God. In support of this conclusion, Jesus' followers experienced a series of visions that they interpreted in the light of their religious tradition: the end was nigh, the resurrection of the dead had begun, "Christ has been raised from the dead, the first fruit of those who have died" (1 Cor 15:20). One of the earliest expressions of this

Christian core message is preserved in a letter from Paul to the Christian community in the city of Corinth, Greece. There Paul restates what their faith is supposed to be all about:

> For I handed on to you as of first importance what I in turn had received: that Christ died for our sins in accordance with the scriptures, and that he was buried, and that he was raised on the third day in accordance with the scriptures, and that he appeared to Cephas, then to the twelve. Then he appeared to more than five hundred brothers and sisters at one time, most of whom are still alive, though some have died. Then he appeared to James, then to all the apostles. Last of all, as to one untimely born, he appeared also to me. (1 Cor 15:3–8)

The royal heir of an ancient dynasty had died for his people according to the Scriptures; he had been raised from the dead; and he had ascended to the heavenly realm of God. Very soon, in the lifetime of this very generation, he would return. All dead would be raised and history as we know it would end in the Last Judgment. Meanwhile, the Christian communities were to remain pure in faith, order, life, and work. This was Paul's message in a nutshell.

Paul had little interest in the historical person of Jesus or his teachings. Every now and then he might appeal to a "command of the Lord" as a source of authority. Mostly, however, his focus was on the present moment and on Christ's imminent return. This is understandable. If you believe your generation will be the last on earth, there is no point in preserving history for posterity. Even more so, as the future will be completely different from the past:

> even though we once knew Christ from a human point of view, we know him no longer in that way. So if anyone is in Christ, there is a new creation: everything old has passed away; see, everything has become new! (2 Cor 5:16–17)

Besides, leaving old things behind served Paul's interests. In his former life, he had been persecuting Christians—especially those who were relaxed about the Jewish ritual law and willing to take the good news outside of the Jewish community. A young Pharisee feeling strongly for the purity of the Jewish way of life, Paul had loathed the Hellenized, cosmopolitan wing of the Jesus movement. Yet he was a different person now—and very conscious of the difference it made. Should someone suggest that members of his congregations (he could be a rather possessive parent to the communities he had fathered) have themselves circumcised or become otherwise observant Jews, he would have absolutely none of that. Instead, he proclaimed that the law of Moses was outdated and unsuitable for Christians. This annoyed his Jewish Christian brothers and sisters unspeakably, and even more so as they did not think much of him in the first place. In their mind, this "apostle of nations" was but an outsider, a self-made man whose late personal encounter with the risen Jesus certainly didn't qualify him to call himself an apostle.

Paul's row with Jewish Christians helps us understand why he downplayed the historical Jesus and focused on the risen Christ instead. Unlike the established leaders of the early Christian movement in Jerusalem, he had never known Jesus "from a human point of view." The authority of Cephas (or, as the nations would come to know him, Peter), John, and James as "pillars" of the Christian community rested—in addition to timely apparitions of the risen Jesus—on the fact that they had followed the Lord during his lifetime. Paul lacked this merit, and there was no way he could acquire it.

Influenced by his background, Paul's teaching became good news to everyone hungry for an equal opportunity and a second chance. Whoever you might have been on whatever basis made no difference, once you became a Christian:

> There is no longer Jew or Greek, there is no longer slave or free, there is no longer male and female; for all of you are one in Christ Jesus. (Gal 3:28)

As you might expect, the Christian communities were soon filled with people for whom their former identities had had little to offer:

> Consider your own call, brothers and sisters: not many of you were wise by human standards, not many were powerful, not many were of noble birth. (1 Cor 1:26)

For these people, their newly found faith was a source of liberation, based on an idea of a common humanity in Christ.

Paradise Lost

While Paul all but ignored the life and teachings of the earthly Jesus, there would soon be others who cared a lot about such things. Between 70 and 100 CE, the four New Testament Gospels came into being. Their authors remain unknown. The titles and epigraphs are of later origin. Ecclesiastical traditions betray a late attempt to secure a link between each Gospel and some apostolic authority: Mark, for example, would have been Peter's personal assistant, Matthew the tax collector mentioned in the Gospel named after him, and so on. In light of modern critical research, however, none of those accounts has much source value. Matthew's narrative contains no reference to the author, nor does Mark's. The short introductory remarks in Luke's gospel and the Acts of the Apostles declare the author's purpose in writing the two books, but that is all. Close to the end of John's gospel, we learn that a favorite disciple of Jesus will claim responsibility for the work, but most scholars consider this a literary device employed to emphasize the trustworthiness of the narrative.

Judging from its contents, Matthew's gospel has a Jewish Christian background. The author portrays Jesus as the Messiah, the Anointed One, whose coming was predicted in the prophetic writings of the Hebrew Bible; he would be not just a legitimate king with a mandate from heaven, but also a new Moses who brings God's law to perfection. Luke, on the other hand, wrote to a Greco-Roman audience. His Jesus is a paragon of virtue and an enlightened teacher of morality. In Mark's dramatic narrative, Jesus' mighty acts of wonder are followed by his inexplicable suffering. An ostensibly biographical work, John's gospel is actually a theological treatment on the perfect unity of God the father and his only son Jesus.

Despite their differences, the evangelists shared common aims. Just as Paul had his reasons to downplay the traditions about the historical Jesus, so did the evangelists have an interest in bringing them to public knowledge.

First, it was becoming evident that Jesus wouldn't return in the immediate future. Therefore, his teachings and the story of his life would have to be preserved for posterity.

Second, giving precedence to the risen Christ at the expense of the earthly Jesus was not without problems. The visions continued; early Christian prophets kept on receiving new instructions from the risen Lord, and a growing number of people considered this heavenly wisdom far superior to whatever Jesus had preached during his lifetime. So, new sayings were added to anthologies of Jesus' teachings. Later, these would be accompanied with a whole new literary genre: post-resurrection dialogues between Jesus and his disciples. Such nouveau traditions eroded the authority of "the twelve" and their heritage. They also threatened the unity of the Jesus movement: different prophets had different visions, and it was becoming increasingly difficult to keep those in harmony. If the apostolic element was to keep control of the movement, the direct connection to heaven had to be shut down. Jesus would no more speak live from above; instead, his voice was to be confined within the limits of a historical narrative. Incarnate in letters, his words would not pass away but remain the same now and forever.

On the other hand, some teachings of Jesus remained as risky for Christians as they had once been for the Nazarene himself. As Christians were moving forward and spreading their good news throughout the Roman Empire, they were keen to show they were good citizens leading a decent life and seeking no trouble with the governing authorities, "for there is no authority except from God, and those authorities that exist have been instituted by God" (Rom 13:1). Yet their Lord was known as the crucified one—that is, a convicted revolutionary—and it was no less than a kind of revolution he had preached:

> Blessed are you who are poor,
> for yours is the kingdom of God.
> Blessed are you who are hungry now,
> for you will be filled.
> Blessed are you who weep now,
> for you will laugh.
> (Luke 6:20–21)

> But woe to you who are rich,
> for you have received your consolation.
> Woe to you who are full now,
> for you will be hungry.
> Woe to you who are laughing now,
> for you will mourn and weep.
> (Luke 6:24–25)

> Truly I tell you, there is no one who has left house or brothers or sisters or mother or father or children or fields, for my sake and for the sake of the good news, who will not receive a hundredfold now in this age—houses, brothers and sisters, mothers and children, and fields, with persecutions—and in the age to come eternal life. But many who are first will be last, and the last will be first. (Mark 10:29–31)

A TRUE STORY?

It was not in the urban centers of Anatolia and the Levant, but in rural Galilee where Jesus met his first followers. His preaching was uncompromisingly radical: in order to survive the impending Last Judgment, you'd need to give up whatever you owned and share it with the poor. Only that would earn you partnership in the coming rule of God. Those who believed left their families and traveled far and wide to spread the news: the end is nigh, so put out your mundane worries and prepare for the greatest reversal of fortunes ever seen.

Yet nothing of that sort ever happened. Instead, the world stayed, and the future belonged to those who were willing to build it for themselves. While holy poverty might remain a valued choice for some, it could never become the norm for mainstream Christianity.

So, what were the options? Well, you could bring in a more spiritual take on Jesus' original message: blessed are the poor *in spirit* (Matt 5:3), for theirs is the kingdom of heaven—immaterial and otherworldly. But this was exactly the point made by those who wanted to drop the awkward Galilean prophet altogether, so that they could freely concentrate on the latest updates from the Lord Christ in heaven. You could hardly beat them at their own game. What you needed instead was an authorized narrative that would establish the original, historical Jesus as the standard source of authority, while also making it clear that any politically radical musings were now yesterday's news. Fortunately, there were capable people available for the job, and the most exemplary of them was Luke.

Luke has a well-established reputation as a friend of the poor and the marginalized. While Mark's action-oriented narrative contains comparatively few teachings of Jesus (although Mark keeps telling us that Jesus was teaching all the time), and while Jesus' main topic in John (whose narrative is nothing but talk) is not God's kingdom but how people may come to know God through Jesus, Luke (as well as Matthew) seems to have made use of an extensive anthology of Jesus' sayings. The compendium itself has not survived; scholars call it "The Sayings Gospel Q" (from the German word *Quelle*, "source"), and, judging from its contents, Jesus certainly had a special affinity with the poor. Moreover, Luke has made use of other sources to bring together plenty of similar material, so that his Gospel is now truly a gospel for the needy.

For all that Luke knew, Jesus said God's kingdom belonged to the poor, and he obliged his followers to give up their possessions for the common good. In the Acts of the Apostles—the second part of Luke's two-volume work—the first Christian community in Jerusalem is keen to walk the talk:

> All who believed were together and had all things in common; they would sell their possessions and goods and distribute the proceeds to all, as any had need. (Acts 2:44–45)

Luke accepted Jesus' revolutionary overtones just as they were handed on to him. In his orderly biblical mind, however, there was a time for every matter under heaven. Radical communism and an itinerant lifestyle obviously had their time as long as Jesus himself and his immediate followers were in charge. After that, a more revisionary approach would come in handy.

It was the German New Testament scholar Hans Conzelmann who first noticed that, in Luke's narrative, history is divided into three parts. The first part, "the time of the law and the prophets," came to conclusion with John the Baptist. It was followed by, first, the time of Jesus' earthly ministry—"the middle of time," as Conzelmann called it—and then, the still-ongoing "time of the church." The key point is that "the middle of time" is now irrevocably in the past. What was current then is no more current today:

> [Jesus] said to [his disciples], "When I sent you out without a purse, bag, or sandals, did you lack anything?" They said, "No, not a thing." He said to them, "But now, the one who has a purse must take it, and likewise a bag. And the one who has no sword must sell his cloak and buy one." (Luke 22:35–36)

Jesus' ascension to heaven marks the end of a mythical era. What was possible when he was here on earth is not possible anymore. From now on, that time will be a lost golden age, a paradisiacal island in history, an ideal to which there is no return. Untainted by our present imperfection, it will stay that way for eternity.

Splendid as Luke's solution was, it wasn't watertight, and others would soon rush in to fill the gaps in history. Numerous new Gospels emerged to fill us in what Jesus taught his disciples during the forty days between his resurrection and ascension, or in the course of some other private moments he spent alone with his closest friends. Some of his disciples—Thomas, for example, or Mary Magdalene—were believed to have been more privileged than others; they would have received secrets others never heard of. This gave their followers—self-appointed as well as those in good faith—ample reason to prefer their own traditions to any other.

Once the gospel had become a narrative, it could be supplemented endlessly. That's the way narratives are. On the other hand, some version would eventually have to be declared as the original. History matters; endless variation is bad for credibility.

History or Myth?

In a sense, the Gospel narratives are genuinely mythical: they picture a once-upon-a-time, a primordial age at the dawn of our Common Era. In those days, incredible things could happen. Now everything is different: the heavens remain closed, and the earth awaits the Lord's return. Mighty wonders and moral austerity have given way to a familiar, "natural" order of things.

Yet the Gospels contain historical material as well and are in that sense different from myths proper. Many sayings of Jesus preserved in the first three New Testament Gospels—Matthew, Mark, and Luke—as well as in the Gospel of Thomas (an early anthology of Jesus' sayings that was discovered in complete Coptic translation in Egypt in the mid-twentieth century), are probably genuine, although it is difficult to sift them from later Christian tradition. (Most scholars are not as convinced about the value of John's gospel as a historical source.) Accounts of Jesus' miracles combine historical knowledge about his work as a popular healer with later Christian imaginings of how his divine might must have shone through even before it burst into full bloom in his resurrection. Such conglomeration of historical traditions and their mythical interpretations is typical of biblical narrative. While myth, as the popular saying goes, is the native tongue of all religion, it is not the only language the Christian Scriptures know. Sometimes this makes them difficult to understand: can one-and-the-same story be both fact and fiction?

Just how accurate should the Gospels be in order to be taken seriously? Ask a biblical literalist, and the answer will be "one hundred percent." Whatever Jesus said or did must have taken place precisely as the Bible says. On the other hand, as many biblical literalists subscribe to biblical views, not only on history, but on common morality and natural sciences as well, they need not assume any fundamental discontinuity between biblical times and the present age. What was good then is equally good now. The ascension changed nothing at all. An extremely vivid—as well as highly dramatic—example of such a seamless union between biblical narrative and present-day life is represented by the serpent-handling Pentecostals who, taking their lead from Mark 16:17 ("these signs will accompany those who believe: . . . they will pick up snakes in their hands"), hold handfuls of venomous snakes in their religious services.

Other people have sought to keep an equal commitment to biblical accuracy, yet adapt it to a modern scientific world view. When the Enlightenment rationalists reasoned there must be a natural explanation for everything reported in the Bible, they, too, insisted on an unbroken continuity between what was then and what is now—although for them, it was not the ancient text but modern empirical science that set the norm. Like the present day literalists, they didn't think for a moment that some biblical accounts were not literally true; it was just that the biblical writers did not understand correctly what they heard or saw. So, when the Bible tells us that Jesus was walking on the sea, what he actually did was stroll on floating logs of wood. Or, when it says that darkness came over the land when Jesus died, this was because a massive sandstorm hid the sun, and so on; for every biblical miracle a natural explanation was to be found. The German nineteenth-century rationalist theologians became famous for their efforts in this field, and the name of H. E. G. Paulus in particular stood out among them.

This approach never turned out as a success, however. From a scholarly perspective, it is now a thing of the past, although in fiction, popular culture, and folklore, classic rationalist explanations of biblical miracles still flourish. In light of modern scholarship, not so much informed by rationalist arguments as by careful source criticism, the biblical stories are not direct eyewitness accounts but religious literature combining historical traditions and mythical imagination. There is therefore no need to explain every biblical account as historically possible.

Besides, in their original context, the biblical miracle stories hardly make sense except as stories about miracles. The biblical writers were not in the business of keeping record of well-timed natural phenomena and furnishing them with misguided explanations. Rather, they were to pass on, give expression to, and reshape genuine *religious* experiences and beliefs: what Jesus was believed to have been, done, and meant, and how this was integrated into experiences of the divine in the present. The same was true of Jesus himself. While we do not know too much about him with much certainty, we do know that he was not a naturalist philosopher preaching timeless secular truths. Most likely, he was a Jewish popular charismatic, a practicing healer and exorcist who, like many others in his time, waited for God's radical intervention in history. The problems later Christians may have had with his excessive supernaturalism or revolutionary politics were not his problems. What he and his first followers believed made perfect sense in their contemporary environment, although it may no more do so in ours.

So, when some people are skeptical about the historical figure of Jesus because he is such an unmistakably mythical character, they, too, have fallen captive to a sort of biblical literalism. Whether Jesus of Nazareth existed or not is not to be assessed on the basis of what the early Christians believed him to have been and done and whether this is credible or not. The Romans believed their emperors were gods and worked miracles, yet the premises that gods do not exist and miracles are impossible hardly allow the conclusion that Roman emperors are fiction. That is simply a bad argument.

The main reason why an overwhelming majority of critical scholars assume there once was a prophet, holy man, wisdom teacher, insurrectionist—a religious personality of some sort or another—called Jesus is the way the earliest traditions about him were received and processed by the first Christians. Decades of meticulous source criticism have brought to light a picture of someone who was definitely a hard sell in the international market of savior figures: a thoroughly Jewish preacher and exorcist who started his career as a disciple of John the Baptist; who proclaimed an imminent end of the world, or a radical social reform, or both; and who was ostracized by his family, abandoned by his followers, and, finally, executed as a common criminal in a manner designed to inflict utter shame and extreme humiliation. Why would anyone first invent a figure like this, and then have immense trouble in explaining him to their audience, or plainly just pretend he was something else entirely? Certainly it must have been the unfortunate village healer who was presented as the eternal word of God and not the other way round.

There is no doubt that the Jesus of the New Testament Gospels—that is, Jesus as the four evangelists understood him—only exists in the Gospel narratives. Yet his character combines no less than two historical truths: one a story of a Jewish charismatic, his life, works, and violent death; the other, the religious experience of a movement that continued in his wake. Neither of these is a product of pure imagination; rather, they each have a history of their own.

For the audience—ancient or contemporary, aged three or older—this peculiar coexistence of myth and history has not always been easy to grasp. Even for a seasoned reader, a Gospel may come as a story like few others. Yet the ostensibly odd combination serves a purpose: it manages a balance between nonnegotiable ideals and an imperfect reality. Encased in the mythical Galilean spring, Jesus' radical message remains intact and inspiring, free from pressures to compromise. While any historical church cannot but suffer the lamentably human nature of its members and officials, Jesus' image and words are safe from corruption. On the other hand, the very same distance protects the church from the most violent utopian visions. Kingdoms named after God yet built by human hands tend to be far from heaven. Fortunately, the Gospels know no other God incarnate than the one who is yet to return, and even the most enthusiastic idealists must keep their patience.

Eternal Truths?

Not only does biblical history bear resemblance to myth. Also, conversely, biblical myths tend to be read as history. The biblical stories of creation, paradise, and the flood, for example, are typical variations of ancient Near Eastern creation myths. Once they took their place in the Bible, however, they became part of what is essentially an historical plot line, extending from the onset of time to the Last Judgment.

In the West, religious truth has come to equal a particular historical narrative. Christian theologians speak of "salvation history," that is, God's premeditated plan, revealed in and guiding the course of history, to save humankind from sin and death. Everything in the Bible is supposed to gain its meaning from this overarching narrative.

While history has increased in value, myth has decreased. In common English usage, myth has become synonymous with an unfounded or false belief: "Now, that is only a persistent myth." Many—Christians as well as others—assume that it is only the historical material in the Bible that counts, whereas myths are primitive and should therefore be rejected.

Originally, however, myth, too, is a true story—albeit the events it recounts never actually happened in some distant point in time. The point is, rather, that they happen all the time, and we can see that with our very own eyes: light and darkness take turns, seasons follow each other, new life is born from death, humans struggle with their inborn limitations.

Mythical truths are eternal and universal. This may come as an alien thought in our postmodern era of pluralism, relativism, and multiculturalism. Myths earnestly suggest there is such a thing as human nature, common to all people of different ages, genders, and colors. This is also why myths—unlike history, which tends to be written by particular people for particular people—can accommodate the thought of a common, shared humanity. In the course of the paradise story, for example, Adam becomes what his name says he is: a human being—sexual, fallible, vulnerable, and mortal. That is the way humans are.

Some people fear we are becoming illiterate to myths. The pioneers of modern fantasy, J. R. R. Tolkien and George Lucas, shared this concern. Pure fictions that *The Lord of the Rings* and *Star Wars* are, Tolkien and Lucas had an outspoken interest in teaching the audience what myths are like and how they communicate. They hoped their stories would help people reconnect with the original, genuine myths of old. Tolkien specifically wished they would revisit the great narrative of Christianity (which he believed was essentially *both* a full-fledged mythology *and* historically true), whereas Lucas was inspired by a motley selection of humanity's common mythical heritage.

Not all myths are the same, however, so it makes a difference which one you choose as your guiding light. Myths can be conservative or radical—they can support the status quo or demand its destruction. The biblical creation story in Genesis is a conservative one: God puts everything in the world in its proper place and notes that "it was good." The moral of the story is that the world is just like it was meant to be. The book of Revelation, on the other hand, is radical: the world has become evil. It must come to an end and be replaced by another one. Whatever is good belongs outside the old world order.

Usually, however, the two visions coexist side by side. The world as God created it was all good, but now it is broken. The paradise is both the alpha and the omega of history, its beginning and its end.

It is in the nature of Christianity to live between paradise and the apocalypse. In so doing, Christians must keep balance between two radically different visions of reality: one contended realism, and another, committed idealism. On the one hand, you should accept the natural reality as given by God and take care of it the best you can. On the other hand, you will need to keep your distance from the present world order and wait for God's kingdom to come. No wonder, then, that in the course of its long history, Christianity has inspired both revolutionaries and reactionaries.

So, is the Bible true? Yes, but in more than just one way, and only seldom in just one way at a time. Stories about our heavenly Father are certainly not fiction (except that sometimes they are, as in the case of Jonah and Job, but even then it doesn't mean they're not dead serious). They are far too historical to be myths, and have far too much myth in them to count as history—which is good, because to mix the two is exactly what is required if you are to tell a story like theirs. In order to tell their truth about Jesus, the evangelists had to combine traditions about his life and teaching on earth with their contemporary Christian experience about him as the risen Lord.

Myth, tradition, history, experience, imagination—they all melt together on the pages of the Bible. That's what makes the Bible timeless and contextual, true and fiction, history and homily, all at the same time. This may sound disappointing to those who expect their Bible to be perfectly inerrant, historically as well as morally. But where would the idea of an absolutely perfect Bible lead us? Wouldn't it make the Bible, and those who put their hope in it, desperately weak and vulnerable? How could all the faith, hope, and love in and out of this world be based on something that cannot take a single human feature, a single sign of imperfection, without becoming worthless, treacherous, and unreliable? Can only the perfect be good—and would anything perfect be good for humans, whose nature it is to be human, and whose natural habitat is human imperfection?

Living in denial and being led by one's fantasy is as bad an approach to the Bible as it is a bad approach to anything. At best, the Good Book has better things to do than feed its readers' personal appetite for unrestricted spiritual satisfaction. Like all our love objects, the Bible deserves to be loved as it is.

On the other hand, those who would like to see Jesus' message as a purely timeless truth with no connection to history will be disappointed, too. Although the Bible is not an accurate historical report, it can only be understood in the light of the historical conditions in which it originated—and, also, in which it is read. As the former Harvard professor and bishop of Stockholm, Krister Stendahl, put it, all those who read the Bible must first find out what the text once meant, and then, what it means now. Sometimes, these are two very different things. It is to this healthy disappointment so vital for an adult religious life—that the Bible was not written to us but to some other audience entirely—I will turn next.

3

An Immigrant God

What's the Picture?

In a popular textbook of biblical studies, New Testament professor David Rhoads asks his readers to imagine they are film directors tasked to create an authentic-looking scene from Jesus' life.[1] His choice of an example is the story about Jesus healing the man with the withered hand:

> Again he entered the synagogue, and a man was there who had a withered hand. They watched him to see whether he would cure him on the sabbath, so that they might accuse him. And he said to the man who had the withered hand, "Come forward." Then he said to them, "Is it lawful to do good or do harm on the sabbath, to save life or to kill?" But they were silent. He looked around at them with anger; he was grieved at their hardness of heart and said to the man, "Stretch out your hand." He stretched it out, and his hand was restored. The Pharisees went out and immediately conspired with the Herodians against him, how to destroy him. (Mark 3:1–6)

What should a film director know—and, correspondingly, what kind of questions should a biblical scholar ask—in order to comprehend this scene? Several questions spring to mind: What did a synagogue look like? Who went there? How did they take part in the service? How were they dressed? What was the Sabbath and how were you expected to observe it? If

---

1. See Rhoads, "Social Criticism."

you failed to do so, would you be punished for that? What did they think of handicapped people, and how would they show it? Who were the Pharisees and why would they want to accuse Jesus? And so on.

Obviously, you will need to know that the Sabbath was—and still is, in the Jewish religion—a day of rest on which every kind of work was strictly forbidden, and that healing was considered to be work. Observing the Sabbath was a major religious obligation, so that neglecting it made you liable to severe punishment. The Pharisees were a popular religious movement committed to making everyday life holy and pure. Therefore, they were adamant that the Jewish purity law be observed. The situation was tense, because the synagogue was not only a house of prayer but also a court of law.

The key question is why the Pharisees did not bring charges against Jesus, although he did heal the man. The answer is that there was no actual work involved. Jesus did not touch the man; he didn't even say "Be healed!" Instead, he simply told the man to stretch his arm, at which point his hand was suddenly restored. Frustrated, the Pharisees had no choice but to back off, which was awkward for them but would amuse those who have sympathy for Jesus.

Films about Jesus make an instructive point of comparison, as they often have been quite far from authentic. The costumes and scenes have drawn their inspiration not so much from the actual living conditions of the ancient Mediterranean as from various ecclesiastical traditions and pious imagination.

Some directors did not even aim for authenticity in the first place. *The Greatest Story Ever Told* by George Stevens portrays landscapes that remind one of classic Westerns, and the film's casting and general atmosphere are of similar type. The film Stevens is mostly remembered for is *Shane*, a heroic epic that many regard as the greatest Western ever made. It is only appropriate that his Jesus should be a lonely hero surrounded by Hollywood stars.

Likewise, the Italian Pier Paolo Pasolini was not looking for an authentic historical setting. Instead, he wanted to find a modern equivalent to the rural Galilee of Jesus' time. *The Gospel According to St. Matthew* was filmed in Southern Italy, and most of the cast were local peasants. The Marxist director was at home with common people and critical of the clerical and political elite.

Quite often, the ancient story and its modern adaptations not only look different but have different ideas altogether. The blond, blue-eyed Jesus of the Hollywood epics is not only a physical but also mental image of an ideal American male. Standing out from the crowd, he is an individualist fighting all alone against a corrupt, decaying system.

The more recent the film, the more psychological the point of view. Community values and common heritage fade into the background, as faith becomes a personal calling. The adequate response to the good news is no more the hope that the people's collective covenant with God be restored, but a personal identity crisis and the subsequent process of growth. Jesus' main conflict is no more with his outer enemies, the demons and the Jewish and the Roman authorities. Instead, he must overcome his own doubts and fears. While God has prepared a cup of fate for him, he must himself choose to drink it. Thus, *The Last Temptation of Christ* by Martin Scorsese features what is a typical Scorsese hero: a self-absorbed misfit who takes a mythical conflict of good and evil personally.

That's Not My Jesus

Modern films about Jesus read the Gospels in the light of modern times and modern culture. The same has been true of other times and other arts as well. In medieval paintings, the biblical characters appear in medieval costumes in a European setting. Literary adaptations of the figure of Jesus have much in common with other characters of their historical period of origin. The cantatas and Passions by Bach sound far from Eastern music. All this contributes to an image of Jesus as one of us. When devout parents instruct their offspring not to do anything Jesus wouldn't, they certainly think the same must be true the other way round as well: Jesus would never do anything they wouldn't accept.

It makes little sense, however, to blame an artist for a historically inaccurate vision of Jesus. It is artists' duty to express the humanity of their own time, and new interpretations of Jesus' story—the greatest story ever told, as Stevens so aptly renamed it—provide artists of all ages with ample material. Sometimes art can increase our awareness of how our ideas of Jesus are mirror images of our own hopes and ideals. This can make us more critical of any doctrine or practice we are told is "biblical."

While artists should be granted artistic freedom, scholars are rightly expected to be critical. Have they been up to their task? Have they duly recognized the profoundly alien nature of the biblical world? This has by no means always been the case. In his classic history of the early modern research on the historical Jesus, Albert Schweitzer (German theologian, master organist, medical doctor, and Nobel Peace laureate) showed how one scholar after another had projected his own favorite philosophies onto the Nazarene.

Schweitzer himself (as well as some of his colleagues, most notably Johannes Weiss) put Jesus firmly in the setting of first-century Judaism. This brought into light a figure who was very different from what philosophically oriented theologians had imagined him to have been. It was not some timeless wisdom he proclaimed, but an imminent end of the world, a coming judgment, God's kingdom on earth. Like many Jewish and Christian figures of his time, he was confident that the day of the Lord, "great and very terrible" (Joel 2:11), was at hand:

> Truly I tell you, this generation will not pass away until all these things [culminating in the coming of the Son of Man in the clouds] have taken place. (Mark 13:30)

His words echoed those of John the Baptist, who came ahead of him:

> Even now the ax is lying at the root of the trees; every tree therefore that does not bear good fruit is cut down and thrown into the fire. (Matt 3:10)

Later, the baton was handed over to Paul:

> For this we declare to you by the word of the Lord, that we who are alive, who are left until the coming of the Lord, will by no means precede those who have died. (1 Thess 4:15)

So, the author of the book of Revelation was not the only biblical writer who had apocalyptic visions. The Gospels and Paul's letters are permeated with a similar world view: once good and evil have fought their final battle, this corrupt world will come to an end, and a small remnant of people will be saved for life everlasting. This will be their compensation for being unduly marginalized because of their faith: "blessed are you who weep now, for you will laugh" (Luke 6:25).

According to Schweitzer and Weiss, Jesus, too, was an apocalyptic prophet. The end he was waiting for never arrived, however, and this made him a tragic figure. God failed to save his Son, and Jesus' cry on the cross, "My God, my God, why have you forsaken me?" (Mark 14:34) had genuine despair in it.

Schweitzer's and Weiss's observations were turning points in research. Doomsday expectations were such an integral part of early Jesus traditions they simply couldn't be ignored anymore.

Not all scholars today, however, would say Jesus was only, or mainly, a preacher of the end of the world. Some think his teachings and way of life were not far from those of the wandering Cynic philosophers, another type well known in the "Galilee of the Gentiles" (Matt 4:15). The Cynics were eloquent cultural critics who provoked their audience with controversial teachings and cheeky behavior. It was not the end of the world, or anything of that sort, they used to preach about; rather, they were in the business of truth, virtue, and the good life. Like Jesus, they were fond of succinct sayings that would silence all objections, and they were equally realistic—or outright cynical—about the lot assigned to them and their followers in an obtuse world. According to Epictetus, the Cynic must "be flogged like an ass, and while he is being flogged he must love the men who flog him, as though he were the father or brother of them all."[2] Many of Jesus' teachings were similar in tone:

> Blessed are those who are persecuted for righteousness' sake, for theirs is the kingdom of heaven.
> Blessed are you when people revile you and persecute you and utter all kinds of evil against you falsely on my account. Rejoice and be glad, for your reward is great in heaven, for in the same way they persecuted the prophets who were before you. (Matt 5:10–11)
>
> Love your enemies and pray for those who persecute you, so that you may be children of your Father in heaven. (Matt 5:44–45)

On the other hand, if Schweitzer was still alive, he would probably snap that a Cynic Jesus—a maverick verbal virtuoso who mocked every variety of establishment—would have been a raving success in any liberal American university campus. Might it not be the case that scholars have once again made Jesus in their own image?

The Orphaned Jew

Doomsday expectations were not the only thing that would make Jesus alien to some modern Christians. He was also an unadulterated Jew.

---

2. Epictetus, *Discourses*, 3.22.54.

Up until the second half of the twentieth century, most Christian theologians portrayed Jesus as a radical religious reformer whose ideas of a merciful God were in a diametric opposition to "oppressive Jewish legalism." Such a portrait, however, entails a very unfair caricature of first-century Judaism.

First of all, in the time of Jesus, Judaism as religion was only in the making. It came in many varieties, of which movements like the one formed by Jesus and his followers was one. In other words, Jesus' teaching and activities were by no means exceptional. On the contrary, they fit quite well in the Judaism of his day. Jesus was not the only rabbi who taught the Golden Rule ("in everything do to others as you would have them do to you," Matt 7:12; cf. Luke 6:31)—his senior contemporary, the famous Rabbi Hillel is known to have produced a similar maxim—and Galilee had a reputation for charismatic wonder-workers.

Take Honi the Circle Maker, for example. Once upon a time, when there was a great drought in the land, Honi made a circle on the ground and said he would sit in there until God would send the rain. First, there was some drizzle, but Honi was not happy with that: "I asked for proper rain," he said to God. A few light showers followed, yet Honi was not satisfied. It was only when it rained steadily that he would step out of his circle.

The Pharisees rebuked Honi for his lack of humility. Aware of his reputation, they likened him to a spoiled child who knows how to wrap his father around his finger. Jesus would have approved:

> Ask, and it will be given to you; search, and you will find; knock, and the door will be opened to you. For everyone who asks receives, and everyone who searches finds, and for everyone who knocks, the door will be opened. Is there anyone among you who, if your child asks for bread, will give a stone? Or if the child asks for a fish, will give a snake? If you then, who are evil, know how to give good gifts to your children, how much more will your Father in heaven give good things to those who ask him! (Matt 7:7–11)

Also in those times in Galilee, there lived a certain Hanina ben Dosa. He, too, might have been among those who "will pick up snakes in their hands and . . . lay their hands on the sick, and they will recover" (Mark 16:17). Indeed, a snake bit him once, when he was immersed in prayer, and he remained unharmed (the snake perished, though). Hanina's prayers were strong enough to heal the son of the great Rabbi Johanan ben Zakkai—after the rabbi himself had first prayed in vain for his child, lying prostrate on the ground for an entire day.

Like Jesus, Hanina healed people from a distance and could feel if the disease had left them. Like Jesus, he despised wealth and would not worry about tomorrow. Both men were more concerned about the purity of the human heart than about traditional dietary regulations.

So, Jesus' public ministry fit quite neatly into the context of his contemporary Judaism. As to the alleged legalism of the Jewish faith, Judaism never regarded the Torah, the law of Moses, as a means of salvation. Instead, it was a gift from God, given freely to his chosen people, so that they could make the most of their covenant with him and the blessings it involved. The only people who actually asserted that enhanced purity and strict observance of the law were essential conditions of eschatological salvation were those who believed that the end was nigh and repentance therefore imperative—in other words, people like the earliest followers of Jesus. Paul's most zealous opponents who taught that "faith apart from works is barren" (Jas 2:20) came from among his fellow Christians.

So, why is there so much harsh criticism of the Jews in general and the Pharisees in particular in the four Gospels? The answer lies in the situation at the time of their writing. In the year 66, a rebellion against Rome broke out in Judea. Upon crushing it four years later, the Romans destroyed the temple of Jerusalem for good. This became a turning point for the Jewish religion. The groups that were close to the temple—the Sadducees, for instance—went extinct. Some other groups, like the Essenes with their strict community rules, vanished in the winds of war. The Pharisees, however, were able to lay the basis for what would in due time become rabbinic Judaism. In accordance with the Pharisaic teaching, holiness was transferred from the lost sanctuary to everyday life. Although the offerings in the temple had ceased permanently, the Jews could still keep their covenant with God by adhering to their God-given way of life. The Pharisaic tradition of the elders would trim that to perfection.

Meanwhile, among Christians, the cosmopolitan, Hellenistic, Roman-friendly wing had grown stronger. There was no going back to the time when the Jesus movement was a conspicuously Jewish phenomenon. While mainstream Judaism was adopting a more cohesive, traditionalist identity, Christians were pushing their limits vis-à-vis their native Jewish faith. It was going to be a divorce, and a quarrelsome one at that. Each party accused the other of spoiling the common heritage. Christians were banished from the synagogue, and those who kept observing the Jewish ritual law became marginalized among Christians in turn.

It is in the context of this conflict that Matthew, in his Gospel, has Jesus lash out at "the scribes of the Pharisees," whereas "every scribe who has been trained for the kingdom of heaven is like the master of a household who brings out of his treasure what is new and what is old" (Matt 13:52). The same conflict also explains why John is so bitter towards "the Jews" while himself being one: "for the Jews had already agreed that anyone who confessed Jesus to be the Messiah would be put out of the synagogue" (John 9:22). Each evangelist put the story in his own context, eager to make sure Jesus' stern words of rebuke would find the appropriate target.

In the great divorce of Jews and Christians, the mother church was given the custody of the baby Jesus. Ever since, she has preferred not to look at those features in the child that would remind her of his father. Instead, she has dressed him in the style of her every latest infatuation, so that the rural Jewish prophet has been turned into a universal, absolute spirit of the Platonic or Hegelian kind. Nevertheless, there is always something alien about the Christian Jesus. This is a challenge for all those Christians who would like to make him exclusively theirs. Jesus' domestic beauty is in the eye of the beholder. In reality, he is of foreign blood.

Honor and Shame

Jesus' religion and ethnic background are part of his original culture. Not only did this culture give him many of his religious ideas, it also profoundly shaped the way he and his followers viewed the world and related to other people. Ancient Mediterranean communities were in many ways different from modern Western societies, and people who lived there would understand many things quite unlike we do today. Perceptions, emotions, actions, beliefs, values, goals for life—all those were and are culturally conditioned. Together they weave themselves into a fabric of unspoken rules that regulate all social behavior. During recent years, a number of scholars have investigated the makings of this historical fabric in the New Testament and cognate literature. They have worked towards an overall picture of how people in the ancient Mediterranean behaved and why. Studies like Bruce J. Malina's *The New Testament World: Insights from Cultural Anthropology* have shed light on many biblical passages that used to baffle modern readers.

The first-century Mediterranean world was *a culture of honor and shame*. Honor was the pivotal value, the essential social capital. Your honor guaranteed that you were reliable and safe to deal with. It secured that people would do business with you, have you marry their offspring, accept your trade and place of accommodation, and let you fulfill your religious obligations. Without honor none of the above could have been taken for granted. It is no surprise, then, that people would defend their honor at all costs.

A woman's honor was particularly precious. If it was lost, the shame would be there for good, and it would bring permanent harm to the entire family. The protection of female honor remains the most conspicuous feature of contemporary societies of honor and shame, too. In the extreme, it becomes manifest in the so-called honor killings, when the family males take the life of the female they think has brought the family shame. In some parts of the globe, this may still be the sad fate of some unfortunate young women who refuse the marriage her family has arranged for her.

In a culture of honor and shame, honor guaranteed people the position in which they were born. The established social order was considered ideal and complete. Honorable people were not into moving up in the ladder (while parvenus did exist, their advent was, as today, regarded as a sign of moral decay). Rather, they would want to consolidate their current status. This was done by acquiring honor in situations in which it was publicly challenged.

The challenge could be positive—someone would bestow a gift on you, or pay you a compliment—or negative, like an insult or taunt. Whatever the way, it was imperative that you respond to it appropriately, like an honorable person should. In the best-case scenario, both parties would win, as in exchanging gifts or forming alliances. Otherwise, one or the other would increase their honor at the other party's expense. Which way it went depended on if the audience—that is, the community members present—thought your response was any good.

In the Gospels, Jesus and his opponents keep challenging each other all the time. While the crowd is watching, they question each other's right to present oneself as a legitimate religious authority (cf. Mark 2:1–3:6):

> The opponents: Why does this fellow speak in this way? It is blasphemy! Who can forgive sins but God alone?

> Jesus: Why do you raise such questions in your hearts? Which is easier, to say to the paralytic, "Your sins are forgiven," or to say, "Stand up and take you mat and walk"?
>
> The opponents: Why does he eat with tax collectors and sinners?
>
> Jesus: Those who are well have no need of a physician, but those who are sick; I have come to call not the righteous but sinners.
>
> The opponents: Why do your disciples not fast?
>
> Jesus: The wedding guests cannot fast while the bridegroom is with them, can they?
>
> The opponents: Look, why are your disciples doing what is not lawful on the Sabbath?
>
> Jesus: The Sabbath was made for humankind, and not humankind for the Sabbath. Is it lawful to do good or to do harm on the Sabbath, to save life or to kill?

In the Gospels, no one can successfully challenge Jesus' honor. On the other hand, you can hardly say the same of his opponents.

Challenge and response always took place among equals. An insult from an inferior or a favor from a superior was not a challenge and required no response other than appropriate disciplinary measures or proper gratitude. There was no transaction of honor involved. In other words, the Gospels imply that Jesus' opponents had no choice but to treat him as their equal, as the community was willing to grant him that honor.

The community was the sole source and keeper of all the honor there was to gain. There was no honor except in the eyes of the community. This is why the challenge and the response had to be public—and, conversely, this is why all public interaction, if it involved people other than family members, came with a challenge. Everyone's position and identity were constantly open to scrutiny. While we moderns may think of ourselves as individuals determined by our choices and personal history, first-century Mediterranean people were what other people perceived them to be. Identities were collective: whatever you did either confirmed the public opinion of what people of your kind tend to be like, or gave reason to revise it. Imagine being introduced with the simple notion that you are a Smith of New York—after all, everyone knows what the New York Smiths are like. In other words, if people stood out, it was not because they were unique but because they represented the realized potential of their family, nation, and species; and if they progressed, that was not a personal accomplishment but their predestined fate.

The Epic Hero

Literature is a mirror of its age. Literary characters are designed so as to make sense in their cultural environment. In the Gospels, Jesus is an epic hero who presents little change and offers few surprises. This is only natural, because more-or-less everyone in the audience is supposed to know who he is and how his story will go.

The first narrative Gospel we know of, the Gospel of Mark, opens with a one-line synopsis: "The beginning of the good news of Jesus Christ, the Son of God." We know the man, we have heard the news, now we will learn how it all began.

A couple of decades later, Luke could start his account of Jesus' life by saying that many had written on the topic already. So, it was a familiar story to the "most excellent Theophilus" (Luke 1:3) and others in Luke's audience who likewise had been instructed about the basics of Christianity. Now they would hear it again from a professional man of letters, presented in an orderly manner and based on the most reliable sources.

Not only did the audience know the story well. It was, essentially, their story; it was about their hero who had made them what they had become and whom they wished to imitate. The evangelists were not in the business to express an original artistic vision. Rather, they were in the service of their communities, tasked to build up a common faith. In their narrative, the Messiah is as the Messiah does.

How could it have been otherwise? In a culture of honor and shame, characterization was bound to focus on the surface, on what is public and visible. While modern characters are all about inwardness, the evangelists preferred public action. Whatever their characters did bore witness to their inherent nature, and wherever they ended up in the narrative served to demonstrate their God-given destiny. A leopard cannot change its spots.

All four Gospels build on a classic plot line. The first half consists of rising action: Jesus demonstrates his irresistible might in astounding miracles and authoritative teaching. In the climactic high point of the story, his true identity is discovered (Peter recognizes that he is the Christ), which leads to reversal and falling action: Jesus must go to Jerusalem, suffer, and die. In the very end, yet another reversal emerges, as God restores Jesus' power, glory, and honor by resurrecting him from the dead.

As Richard Walsh has noted in a fine study on the Bible and film, modern people have mostly lost their sense of epic. Therefore, they find Jesus nonheroic.

Indeed, modern culture cherishes a different realism. Today's heroes remain incomplete, and their future is always open. Fate is not the key; the persons themselves are. They have no destiny. Instead, they are doomed to choose who they will become.

A world of self-generating characters is a world of individuals. It consists not of stock types but of enigmatic figures constantly in the process of becoming who they are. Perception, development, and growth all take place on the inside. What is private is real, whereas appearances are not to be trusted. As each individual sees the world in his or her own personal way, modern narratives will not reinforce a common faith but foster an ongoing revaluation of all values.

A Different Jesus

The Christian church was not born modern, so it is no surprise if it should find it difficult to embrace modern ways. In depth, it is not so much the usual suspects—such as liberal mores or increased knowledge—that present an issue. Rather, the key question concerns anthropology, that is, the idea of human nature. The ancient Christian heroes are unrecognizable as heroes today.

As presented in the Gospels and proclaimed by the church, Jesus is an epic hero—a living guarantee of an established, eternal set of values. This makes him very different from our contemporary heroes with whom we identify because of their human limitations. We love them because their heroism is not put up for our adoration or to prop up a common ideal. We connect with them because we think they are one of us.

It is not that modern times would not recognize Jesus as a potential hero. The idea of God becoming a man certainly presents a strong promise of shared humanity. "Behold the man," a son of humanity, this is what he looks like!

But does Jesus live up to the promise? In the eyes of a first-century Mediterranean audience, this was no doubt the case. The greatest hero ever seen, Jesus was an epitome of virtue, a human ideal in the flesh. Today, however, things look different. Shared humanity has come to mean a common ground based on everyday experience. This is why the audience will cling to any random human feature Jesus would show—the tears at Lazarus' tomb, his momentary weakness in Gethsemane, any implication that he and Mary Magdalene had some romantic involvement. We want to know how Jesus felt, so that we can become convinced of his true humanity.

Yet there are only few cracks in Jesus' façade. This is why, as Walsh points out, so many Jesus films are about someone other than Jesus. They relocate his story in a new environment, or replace his original character with an imaginary Christ-figure—a character whose life, works, or the impression they make on other people remind us of Jesus. Among the most representative examples of this latter category is Stuart Rosenberg's *Cool Hand Luke*, a classic prison drama bristling with biblical allusions and starring Paul Newman as a mystery convict whose nonviolent resistance makes him immortal in the memory of his fellow inmates. Another fascinating film, *Jesus of Montreal,* by the Canadian director Denys Arcand, tells the story of an uncompromising theatre director who, while working on a play on the Passion of the Christ, becomes all the more Jesuslike. Both films feature a central conflict between an honest individual and a corrupt system. Not only do they tell the story from the point of view of the individual. Individualism is also their main theme and, consequently, the true nature of Jesus' heroism.

Yet another approach, highly typical of modern literature, is to pick someone who was originally a minor character in the Gospels—like Mary Magdalene, Pontius Pilate, or Judas Iscariot—and transform him or her into the narrator-protagonist of the story. Mary Magdalene's point of view, for example, would let us see the events through a woman's eyes. Moreover, it could serve to suggest that Jesus, too, was a sexual being like anyone else in the modern, post-Freudian world.

Sometimes, film producers have upgraded the role of female characters for more opportune reasons: in the early years of filmmaking, when censorship was tight, characters like Mary Magdalene, Salome, or Judith gave directors leeway to portray erotic scenes, and quite a few of them did seize the opportunity.

Yet ironically, early traditions about Mary Magdalene presented her as an example of transcending one's sexuality:

> Simon Peter said to them, "Let Mary leave us, for women are not worthy of life." Jesus said, "I myself shall lead her in order to make her male, so that she too may become a living spirit resembling you males. For every woman who will make herself male will enter the kingdom of heaven."[3]

3. Gospel of Thomas 114.

For those early Christians who looked up to Mary Magdalene as their role model, she was an archetype of immaterial spirituality. In those times, this was regarded as a male quality. It was unusual, so it was thought, that such a highly developed form of human potential as spirituality should materialize in a woman's body.

So, the ancient, spiritually gifted Mary Magdalene stood out as masculine, whereas modern authors are keen to emphasize her feminine, physical sexuality. In a way, both interpretations propose an alternative to their contemporary sexisms—and would appear as suspicious to each other. A modern reader might ask why femininity should be inferior, so that a woman would strive to become a man. A second-century reader, on the other hand, might be bewildered that her twenty-first-century sisters still like to be portrayed mostly as lovers and spouses. Can't they be disciples and apostles quite regardless of their gender?

The Gospel of Judas

As Jesus' significant other, Mary Magdalene is the perfect voice for our postsecular, individualistic age. It is no wonder that since the late twentieth century her figure has become increasingly prominent in literary adaptations of the gospel story. Shortly before, during the two world wars and the Cold War era, it was Judas and Pilate who enjoyed a similar favor. Two great outsiders, they had natural appeal to a generation who like them had put down their God and now felt alone and guilty.

The great Danish philosopher Søren Kierkegaard once remarked, "One will get a deep insight into the state of Christianity in each age by seeing how it interprets Judas."[4] In the modern age, books inspired by *The Gospel of Judas* abound. This mid-second-century Gnostic writing was for a long time known only from a quote by Irenaeus, the bishop of Lugdunum in Gaul (presently Lyon, France). Then, in 2006, *National Geographic* magazine acquired a full Coptic translation (from some group of fishy antiques dealers, as the story goes).

The Gospel of Judas features Judas as Jesus' most trusted disciple who, on Jesus' direct order, helps his soul break free from the prison of the material body. The idea fits well in Gnostic thinking, characterized by a strong contrast between the material world and a higher spiritual reality. According to the Gnostic myth, humankind was originally pure of spirit. In creation,

---

4. Quoted in Pyper, "Modern Gospels of Judas," 115.

however, humans became captive to the matter and lost consciousness of their true nature. In order to be saved from this despicable condition, they had to receive the redeeming knowledge—in Greek, *gnosis*—of who they were and where they belonged.

Before the ancient text was found, many a modern writer had already imagined what the lost Gospel might have contained. Books with titles like *The Gospel of Judas, The Gospel According to Judas, The Lost Testament of Judas Iscariot, The Book of Judas, The Memories of Judas*, and so on, would fill a small bookshelf. Typically, they portray Judas at least as much as the betrayed than as the betrayer. Other people would have misled him with their illusions or false promises, or he deceived himself to believe Jesus was something he, as it turned out, obviously was not. Later, Judas' story would be forgotten, distorted, or written down by others in disregard of what he had to say. The canonical evangelists had no interest in who he really was and why he did what he did. They would make his story another piece of their propaganda, just as he himself was only a pawn in the game of the Jewish and Roman authorities and, eventually, of God himself.

It is hardly a coincidence that so many modern remakes of the betrayer's story originated in times when totalitarian regimes were rampant in Europe. While the Enlightenment and modernization had given people a new sense of inner freedom, government control made sure they nevertheless had little say over their lives. Indeed, the gravest violation of Judas' humanity was that he was not allowed to choose who he would be. His fall from grace down to the bottom of Hell, next to the devil himself, was prepared for him in advance. The Scriptures had to be fulfilled.

According to the British biblical scholar Hugh S. Pyper, the modern literary figure of Judas typically has two options in defense of his humanity. The first is mutiny: the betrayer becomes a Promethean type who fights, either alongside Jesus or in defiance of him, against divine tyranny all the way down to the bitter end. In the second version, Judas is a Kafkaesque character. Adrift in the stream of events, he nonetheless maintains an accurate perception of what is happening to him. He tells his story in the hope that future audiences will recognize him as one of their kind, an image of humanity.

In both cases, Judas is very much the opposite of the man he is in the canonical Gospels. Originally, each evangelist added to his gradual dehumanization. In Matthew's version, Judas used to be Jesus' friend (26:50); first driven by greed, he is later hit by remorse. In Luke's gospel,

Satan corrupts Judas and has him destroyed completely and horribly. John, finally, makes the most out of the theme of predestination. His Judas is a puppet on a string, caught in the eternal battle between cosmic forces beyond his control:

> So when [Jesus] had dipped the piece of bread, he gave it to Judas son of Simon Iscariot. After he received the piece of bread, Satan entered into him. Jesus said to him, "Do quickly what you are going to do." Now no one at the table knew why he said this to him. Some thought that, because Judas had the common purse, Jesus was telling him, "Buy what we need for the festival"; or, that he should give something to the poor. So, after receiving the piece of bread, he immediately went out. And it was night. (John 13:26–30)

In the New Testament Gospels, Judas loses his humanity and becomes demonized instead. In modern literature, it is the other way round: the notorious betrayer, given the opportunity to tell his story, turns out to be an ordinary human being after all.

Even still, Judas and Pilate remain the ones who killed God. This helps explain why they were in such vogue at the high point of secularization between and shortly after the two world wars. Their stories became the authoritative creation myths of the modern, post-Nietzschean, godless humanity. They were destined to send God Incarnate to the cross, despite their doubts and second thoughts. Like them, the modern secularized men and women would learn that there were no grounds for their faith; that religion was outdated and had to be dropped; that God was dead for good, that humans had slain him. Yet this did not make them feel triumphant, but sad. Like Judas, they wept at the innocence lost. Like Pilate, they were disturbed by the thought they had to condemn the Son of God to death. Of all biblical characters, it was Judas and Pilate whose experiences were closest to theirs. Disenchanted, modern humanity was surprised by loneliness.

✦

The many variants of Jesus' story show how each age remakes the Good Book in its own image. The illusion of timelessness is based on endless variation. The Bible is taken to represent and endorse whatever culture, values, and world view each generation of readers should regard as natural and take for granted.

On the other hand, there is no going back to any "original Jesus." A strictly first-century Savior would not work today. You cannot remove him from his original setting and insert him in an entirely different world where his words would have a different meaning altogether.

Nor does it make sense to put the ancient biblical culture up as a norm. There is a sound case for such things as secular medical science and women's suffrage, even though they would have been an anathema where Jesus came from. Also, as Walsh astutely points out, the quest for an authentic Jesus is yet another case of modern individualism. In order to stand out from the crowd, we prefer the latest, critically acclaimed scholarly update of Jesus to any old, common church tradition. But is the man in the mirror really the Galilean himself?

Eventually, the Jesus of the Gospels is not to be found from behind the narrative but within and in dialogue in it. The same is true of other biblical characters. Perhaps the reason why they endure time so well is because they shed their skin endlessly?

4

So Much Out of So Little

Everything You Need to Know

The mystery of biblical characters is the mystery of the mustard seed: how does so much come out of so little? Considering the very few verses about Judas, Pilate, or Mary Magdalene, it is astonishing how many legends and stories have later emerged about them. As noted by the great late English critic Frank Kermode, the Bible provides the best examples of how little it takes to make a character. "A few indications of idiosyncrasy, of deviation from type," and there they are: the anguished betrayer, throwing away the stained silver; the baffled ruler haunted by his conscience; the desolate disciple looking for her master's body.[1]

Another gifted reader of biblical literature, Robert Alter, would even go so far as to see the very first seeds of modern psychological realism planted in biblical characters. As those seeds would grow, the age of great epics would gradually give way to a new kind of literary hero, unpredictable and open to change.

Be that as it may, biblical characterization is notoriously sparse. The audience will only learn so much as it needs to know. So, we have no information at all, say, about what Jesus looked like. We do know, however, that Esau was a hairy man (so we will understand what his smooth-skinned

---

1. Kermode, *The Genesis of Secrecy*, 98.

twin brother Jacob was up to when he tied goatskins around his arms and neck before asking their poor blind father Isaac for a blessing); we learn that Bathsheba was very beautiful (so it is no wonder that king David should fall for her); and we gather that Zacchaeus was short (which is why he had to climb a tree to see Jesus). Such personal features would make no difference as such; they only matter insomuch as they contribute to the plot and the moral of the story. In this sense, the biblical narrative is like a well-told joke, whose every single feature is directed towards the punch line.

The Bible's sparseness in giving any formal portrayal of characters is quite different from the Greek epics. Homer invested extensively in the depiction of his heroes and their environment. In his 1946 modern classic, *Mimesis: The Representation of Reality in Western Literature*, Erich Auerbach made a well-known comparison of these two varieties of ancient literary art.

In *The Iliad* and *The Odyssey*, Auerbach wrote, all focus is on the foreground. People and settings are illustrated in great detail. Everything that matters is on display and immediately accessible to the reader. The characters are transparent, their interior life is open for us to examine, and their nature equals the sum total of their visible characteristics.

Not so in the Bible. Time and again, the Hebrew Scriptures—and it is the Hebrew Bible Auerbach is discussing at this point—hide their essential meanings underneath their surface, so that it becomes the readers' duty to bring them into the daylight. Given only sparse and ambiguous information, the readers have to infer, make guesses and interpretations, and correct those guesses and interpretations whenever their expectations are not fulfilled in the course of the narrative. In Auerbach's own words, constant retention and suggestiveness make the biblical narrative "fraught with background": "Since so much in the story is dark and incomplete, and since the reader knows that God is a hidden God, his effort to interpret it constantly finds something new to feed upon."[2]

Auerbach took as an example one of the most disturbing stories in the Bible, namely God's command that Abraham sacrifice his beloved son Isaac. The narrative in Genesis 22 is extremely dense, even by biblical standards. One simple clause follows another. The focus is exclusively on action. There is no redundant detail to distract the reader, even momentarily, from the utmost anxiety of the scene.

---

2. Auerbach, *Mimesis*, 15.

First, God and Abraham meet in an unknown location. Geography and setting are unimportant. What counts is Abraham's moral position in respect to God, who has called to him, and Abraham answers: "Here I am," waiting for your command.

While Homer would describe vividly the bodily form and the manner of entrance of each Olympian god, the biblical deity is the indescribable himself. His name is not to be spoken; no one shall see him and live. Besides, his looks are irrelevant; when God and humanity meet, everything external is left aside.

After the austere opening, Abraham and Isaac begin their journey to the land of Moriah (you are free to imagine the landscape). They travel for three days (and whatever happened during those three days is of no importance). Abraham has a donkey, two servants, wood, fire, and a knife (and not a word is used to describe them). As to Isaac, we learn that Abraham loved him. That is all that matters.

The dialogue is sparse, too. As Auerbach points out, what the characters say does not reveal their thoughts but hides them. God will not tell Abraham why he wants Isaac sacrificed. When Isaac asks about the missing lamb, Abraham tells him to leave that to God.

"So the two of them walked together," father and son, in silence, according to God's obliging command. Their particularity has vanished; their identity makes no difference. They are the universal Parent and Child—precious to each other, at the mercy of their destiny. Just as the biblical God refuses to be an inanimate idol, so Abraham and Isaac are not crafted images of humanity. Rather, they embody humanity itself, its smallest common denominator, purged of everything but what is immediately recognizable to all people of all times.

The Reader Makes the Story

Scant illustration is something the biblical stories have in common with the joke. Yet the Bible and the joke are designed to evoke a very different response. The joke is never to be explained. If you need to do that, you are one bad comedian. The history of biblical reception, on the other hand, is all about interpretation and exegesis. Innumerable sages and scholars have read most sublime meanings into the minutest details of the sacred text.

Not that there wasn't an occasional debate on the limits of reasonable interpretation. In his witty and entertaining account of rabbinic exegesis,

Reading the Book: Making the Bible a Timeless Text, Burton L. Visotzky recounts an influential dispute between two second-century Jewish luminaries, Rabbi Aqiba and Rabbi Ishmael.

For Rabbi Ishmael, "the Torah speaks in human discourse"; like everyday speech, the Scripture, too, contains plenty of random expressions. Therefore, it makes no sense to give equal weight to every word. It is the content that matters, not the way of expression. The story of Abraham and Isaac, for example, is, above all, a lesson in obedience.

Rabbi Aqiba could not disagree more. After all, the Scripture is the word of God; how could there be anything redundant in it? Certainly, every excess must have a special meaning.

Rabbi Aqiba was not alone with his view. Consider what a Rabbi Jesus taught about the Torah in his Sermon on the Mount:

> For truly I tell you, until heaven and earth pass away, not one letter, not one stroke of a letter, will pass from the law until all is accomplished. (Matt 5:18)

In historical terms, it was Rabbi Aqiba who won the day. On the Christian side, the Alexandrian school of allegorical interpretation overcame the literalist exegetes of Antioch. "There is nothing in the Scripture superfluous," says Origen; "In the divine Scriptures every word, syllable, accent and point is packed with meaning," says Jerome.[3] All you need is an avid sense of symbolism—a talent the church fathers put to frequent use. In order to understand the Hebrew Bible, they consulted the Christian New Testament. As Jesus carried his cross, wrote Augustine, so Isaac carried the wood for his sacrifice; and who was the ram, caught in the thicket by its horns, if not Jesus, crowned with thorns?

While the heydays of allegorical interpretation were over by early modern times, God remains in the details. Preachers, scholars, and commentators keep expounding the Scriptures verse by verse, word by word, accent by accent. Rabbi Ishmael was fighting the windmills. With a work as dense, enigmatic, and revered as the Bible—as fraught with background, as Auerbach would say—there is no end for interpretation.

The holier the text, the more extensive the exegetical industry. As sacred texts in particular are believed to bristle with meaning, they rapidly become dependent on trained commentators. Jesus subscribed to this, too:

---

3. Quoted in Visotzky, *Reading the Book*, 18.

> And he said to them, "To you has been given the secret of the kingdom of God, but for those outside, everything comes in parables" (Mark 4:11).

God speaks in riddles only a few can crack. Yet this was not always so. In fact, Rabbi Ishmael was only taking God at his own word:

> Surely, this commandment that I am commanding you today is not too hard for you, nor is it too far away. It is not in heaven, that you should say, "Who will go up to heaven for us, and get it for us so that we may hear it and observe it?" Neither is it beyond the sea, so that you should say, "Who will cross to the other side of the sea for us, and get it for us so that we may hear it and observe it?" No, the word is very near you; it is in your mouth and in your heart for you to observe. (Deut 30:11–14)

The Art of Reticence

Reading literature is an art of imagining the unsaid. No story succeeds in telling everything. A competent reader will know how to fill in the gaps.

Some narratives are more open ended than others, leaving quite a few things for the reader to imagine. Sometimes this is due to the storyteller's lack of skill, so that essential information is missing and the narrative becomes difficult to understand. On the other hand, modern writers and critics in particular value a diversity of meanings, as that is seen to give a more adequate portrayal of the polyphonic, dialogical nature of all human reality.

The biblical narrative typically has many gaps the reader should fill in. This is not always intentional but results from a long history of composition. Biblical writers made use of oral and written sources, and many biblical books have gone through extensive revision. Subsequent writers have supplemented each other's work by inserting new material, omitting what they felt was inappropriate, introducing commentary, and so on. So it is only natural that the text should contain redundancies, inconsistencies, and gaps.

On the other hand, the biblical narrators are quite keen on reticence and quite intent on engaging their readers. It becomes the readers' task to complete the story, and they learn that reality does not yield meaning easily. This could hardly be otherwise: after all, God is a hidden God, and while he may have made human beings straightforward, they have devised many schemes (Eccl 7:29).

A number of literary critics—Robert Alter, for example—argue that biblical characterization goes hand in hand with the biblical understanding of humanity. As in real life, so in the Bible people's intentions come into light only gradually, so that it is difficult to reach a conclusive judgment on them. Far from complete, biblical characters always retain potential for change. Therein they differ from the Greek epic heroes famous for their fixed epithets. Unlike "resourceful Odysseus," Jacob is not "wily Jacob," nor is Moses "sagacious Moses."[4] Rather, they are God's children at their most typical: what they will be has not yet been revealed (1 John 3:2).

In their by now classic analysis of biblical characterization, the Israeli critics Menahem Perry and Meir Sternberg focused on David's unfortunate fling with Bathsheba in 2 Samuel 11. The question raised by this instructive narrative is, what kind of man is David? The answer will depend on your reading of the story. The narrator keeps a marked distance at all times, and maintains what is often a significant silence.

The story opens with subtle irony. It is spring, the time when kings go out to battle, yet this king is happy to send his general, his officers, and indeed "all Israel" to war, while he remains comfortably at Jerusalem. Late in the afternoon, he lifts himself from the couch, goes for a walk on the roof of his palace, and sees from there a woman bathing. We are told that "the woman was very beautiful," yet we learn nothing about David's thoughts or emotions. This is why what happens next will present us with more questions than answers. David makes inquiries about the woman; learns that she is called Bathsheba and is married to Uriah the Hittite; has her brought into his palace, sleeps with her, and sends her away.

Did David fall in love at first sight, and did that disturb his judgment? Or did he simply take advantage of the woman at hand? The reticent narration leaves it all open—although it is, admittedly, the very same reticence that makes the latter interpretation sound more probable. David saw a naked woman, invited her to his house, had sex with her, and sent her away. That is all, as there really isn't anything else to tell.

Next, David learns that the woman is pregnant. The narrator will not say who the father is, yet we may infer it from what was told earlier: she had just purified herself after her period when she arrived at David's house.

Then David summons Uriah the Hittite to Jerusalem. Again, we are left wondering what the king is up to. There are several options, each of which will show him in a slightly different light. Will he confess what he

---

4. Alter, *The Art of Biblical Narrative*, 126.

has done? Will he apologize? Or does he think he can bribe or intimidate Uriah to remain silent?

David's true intentions are only revealed gradually. Ostensibly, he is using every means at his disposal to befriend Uriah. He asks him how the war is going; he gives him a present, invites him to dinner, and grants him leave to visit his wife. In reality, as the reader will no doubt soon figure out, David's only purpose is to get the poor man to sleep with his wife so that her pregnancy should not come as a surprise. Yet this will not work out, as Uriah vows astonishing solidarity with his comrades and the country he serves:

> The ark and Israel and Judah remain in booths; and my lord Joab and the servants of my lord are camping in the open field; shall I then go to my house, to eat and to drink, and to lie with my wife? As you live, and as your soul lives, I will not do such a thing. (2 Sam 11:11)

Twice, David tells Uriah to go home. The second time, he even makes sure the man is properly drunk. Yet it is all to no avail. Uriah will not go down to his house but sleeps at the door with the servants.

Uriah's outstanding sense of honor casts an even darker shadow on David's actions: my, the king *is* home and eats and drinks and sleeps with other men's wives! But is the sting intentional, and is Uriah really the great idealist he would seem to be? Or is it possible that he has learned of his wife's infidelity and pregnancy? The reader may want to consider that option. In all likelihood, both David and the reader were surprised to learn that Uriah failed to go home. When David first sent him off to his wife, he did not protest at all. It is only when the king learns that he slept at the entrance of his palace and asks for explanation, that he replies with words that assert his honor and put shame on David. Is that on purpose?

As the question remains open, the reader is left with two alternative interpretations. Each of them leaves David in disgrace, yet in a different way. If Uriah is a loyal soldier acting in good faith, then David's scheming is ruthless and cowardly. If, on the other hand, David is challenged by an offended husband, then the situation is but awkward and shameful.

In the morning, David writes a letter to Joab and sends it off together with Uriah. David's instructions are to have Uriah killed in the battle.

What goes on there in David's mind? Again, the reader has several options to ponder. Neither David nor the reader can be sure if Uriah knows about David's affair with Bathsheba or not. Nor can the reader tell what the king is thinking.

If David believes that Uriah is acting in good faith, his primary goal will be to marry Bathsheba as soon as possible, so as to avoid a scandal. In other words, what we are about to witness is not a crime of passion but evasion of responsibility. David will marry Bathsheba, because he has no other choice.

On the other hand, if David believes that Uriah knows about Bathsheba's pregnancy, the scandal is already in the air. Someone has been talking, and it is only a matter of time before the whole of Jerusalem knows. In this case, David's actions seem less calculated. Once his spontaneous efforts at a cover-up fail, he gets rid of the man who stands in his way and marries the woman he wants.

As David's emotions and motives go unmentioned, the reader may (or better, must) choose between different interpretations. Each choice will further contribute to David's character. Although some assumptions will be confirmed in the course of the narrative, David's figure remains ambiguous. Thus the story gives yet another dramatic account of the biblical truth with which God declared David as king: "the Lord does not see as mortals see; they look on the outward appearance, but the Lord looks on the heart" (1 Sam 16:7). And indeed it is God who, eventually, gives the only conclusive judgment on David's action: "But the thing that David had done displeased the Lord" (2 Sam 11:27).

Coming-of-age

Bathsheba wasn't David's destiny, nor was it inevitable that David should murder Uriah. Surrounded by epic heroes as they may be, the readers of the second book of Samuel will learn that life nonetheless involves making choices that both reveal character and give it further shape. You can't undo your past history, and if other people should fail to hold you accountable, at least God will. He will know who you truly are.

On the other hand, the future always remains open, and the Lord is a merciful God. As long as there is life, everything and everyone is still in the making. Therefore, no one should be judged prematurely. God only knows the human heart, so we should leave the last judgment to him.

It is astonishing how often the biblical narrative reads as a coming-of-age story. This is probably why certain biblical characters feature in so many children's books and films. A children's writer and scholar of children's literature, Jennifer Rohrer-Walsh, has made an informative analysis of the DreamWorks animated film *The Prince of Egypt*. How does the cinematic adaptation of Moses' coming-of-age differ from the original biblical story in Exodus?

A typical coming-of-age story follows the pattern of the rite of passage: *separation* is followed, first, by *transition*, and then, *incorporation* (at this point, Rohrer-Walsh follows Arnold van Gennep). In the separation stage, the protagonist is reckless. No more a child yet not quite an adult, the future hero breaks boundaries and ignores norms. This can only continue for so long, as the community will not tolerate such behavior. The protagonist must leave the childhood home for a temporary exile, so as to grow into a new role and build up a new identity.

As old ways will not work in a new environment, obstacles and ordeals are bound to emerge. Children's literature and youth fiction are packed with championship games, encounters with the opposite sex, moral conflicts, and personal losses. J. K. Rowling's Harry Potter plays Quidditch, falls in love, comes to know good and evil, and mourns people and things that life takes away from him.

In trials and tribulations, the protagonist is supported by a mentor. Mentor figures are often eccentric and may even appear hostile at first. Yet they develop a relationship of trust with the protagonist, guiding the young hero to learn from experience, take advice, and think of the consequences of every action.

Mentor figures tend to be old, alienated, and somewhat unattractive. Yet they are wiser and more patient than the protagonist, and therefore qualified to show the way through the transitional stage. Then their work is done, and the hero must proceed to the incorporation stage alone.

In the end, the hero is a full member of the grown-up community. The degree of the hero's independence will depend on the difficulty of the ordeals passed. The greater the obstacles, and the more alone the hero was when they faced them, the more independent and accountable an adult the hero will be. On the other hand, if the transition was assisted with plenty of external support, the hero will become a dependent adult, readily relying on the community for help.

Coming-of-age stories concentrate on the individual. It is the individual's personal growth that is in focus, even though the goal is incorporation in the community. As Rohrer-Walsh notes, herein lies the greatest difference between modern stories and the biblical narrative. In the Bible, the individuals only count so much as they are guardians, patriarchs, or archetypes of a particular community. The stories of Abraham, Jacob, Joseph, and Moses are not concerned with each person's self-fashioning but with Israel's path into a covenant with God. Likewise, David's adventures are of no interest as such; we only learn of them because they involve the beginnings of an eternal dynasty of which the future redeemer will be born.

Yet even still, despite this fundamental difference, the many similarities and points of contact between the Bible and the coming-of-age story remain. The biblical heroes are best remembered for their personal histories on which generations of pious readers have modeled their spiritual journey.

The typical pattern repeats itself, for example, in the stories about the patriarchs in Genesis. First, all that was before must be left behind. Abram is to go from his country and his kindred and his father's house to a foreign land; Jacob will escape from Esau's fury to Canaan; Joseph's brothers sell him to slavery in Egypt. In two cases out of three, the protagonist's behavior betrays his immaturity: the young Jacob does not hesitate to cheat his father, brother, and uncle, and his son Joseph is vain and arrogant.

The transition stage is rife with tribulations in a foreign land. Joseph finds himself in prison; Jacob's nocturnal wrestling with a stranger at Peniel is one of the most well-known allegories of human struggle for growth; and, as we saw shortly before, the Lord's testing of Abraham is the mother of all tribulation stories in the history of Western literature.

The biblical mentor figure is no less than God himself (although he may not always be immediately recognizable for who he is). He reminds the hero of his reliability in the days of old, gives valuable advice, and sheds light on the future. As appropriate of a mentor, he can be mysterious, capricious, and antisocial: he will indeed attack both Abram and Jacob once.

Properly tested, the hero will obtain a new identity: Abram becomes Abraham, Jacob is renamed Israel, and the Pharaoh gives Joseph the name Zaphenath-paneah. They will also be incorporated in the community: Jacob and Esau reconcile, and Joseph is reunited with his brothers. The fact that Joseph bears them no grudge is a sign of his maturity. He can see beyond his own needs and attends to the needs of others:

> Even though you intended to do harm to me, God intended it for good, in order to preserve a numerous people, as he is doing today. So have no fear; I myself will provide for you and your little ones. (Gen 50:20–21)

David's history, too, shows occasional features of the coming-of-age story. At the entrance of the future king, the focus is on his adolescence: in human eyes, the youngest of Jesse's eight sons may seem an unlikely choice. Yet the Lord knows what is in the heart of the young shepherd.

The testing begins when David encounters the giant warrior Goliath. Neither the enemy nor his own people take him seriously yet. His eldest brother Eliab is angry to find him in the military camp asking questions about "this uncircumcised Philistine" and the reward for the man who kills him:

> Why have you come down? With whom have you left those few sheep in the wilderness? I know your presumption and the evil of your heart; for you have come down just to see the battle. (1 Sam 17:28)

David answers just like a teenager would:

> What have I done now? It was only a question. (1 Sam 17:29)

Even Goliath does not find David much of an opponent:

> When the Philistine looked and saw David, he disdained him, for he was only a youth, ruddy and handsome in appearance. The Philistine said to David: "Am I a dog, that you come to me with sticks?" (1 Sam 17:42–43)

Yet David, armed with a mere sling and stones, takes him down cheerfully. Other victories follow, and David becomes a hero loved by the people and respected by his comrades. This fills King Saul with envy. In a paranoid frenzy, he tries to take David's life.

Escaping Saul's persecution is the most demanding of David's trials. Therein he is helped by Saul's daughter Michal and Saul's son Jonathan, which increases the feel of generational conflict in the story.

The transition stage echoes the fate of the patriarchs: fleeing from Saul, David must leave the country for an itinerant life. For some time, he even camps with the enemy, the Philistines. Along the way, others in distress join him in hundreds. As their captain, David grows into a leader and prepares to assume kingship.

Yet David's coming-of-age never comes to a final conclusion. The struggle to become a responsible adult continues even after his enthronement, as the Bathsheba incident and the ensuing moral conflicts illustrate. The revolt of his son Absalom temporarily recasts David into the role of an itinerant refugee. On his deathbed, the former warrior king is weak and easily manipulated. Although the days are gone when he could make sexual advances, a beautiful servant girl is brought in to keep him warm. For David, as for so many biblical characters, personal growth takes a lifetime and even then is still unfinished.

The Disappearing God

Why are biblical coming-of-age stories so often incomplete? First of all, it may be an entirely different story that the biblical narrators had in mind. David, for example, is not so much a spiritual model for the reader as a national hero and a founder of a dynasty. Second, biblical stories are different, because they feature God as the mentor figure. While a standard mentor would fade into the background as the hero gains independence, God's providence will continue forever. As consoling a thought as that may be, does it also mean that you cannot grow independent of God? Is faith a form of addiction?

In addition to individual coming-of-age stories, there is also an overarching story line that extends from the creation story, first, to Moses and the giving of the law, and then, in the Christian Bible, to the assumption of Christ. As both Jack Miles and Richard Elliot Friedman have pointed out, the Hebrew Bible tells the story of a disappearing God. The Almighty gradually leaves the earth and finds a new residence in heaven. Likewise, the Gospels are literature of renunciation: Jesus' followers need to accept that he must go away. The mythic Galilean spring is to be transformed into reality as we now have it, uncompromising and nonnegotiable. What results is a twofold coming-of-age story. On the one hand, God finds his proper place and role as a transcendent, otherworldly being. On the other hand, people are expected to cope with a reality that involves frustration and suffering.

In the opening narratives of Genesis, God and humanity are simultaneously present in one space. It takes no special revelation to bring them together. Neither party has to leave its own reality to enter the reality of the other. In paradise, God's world and the world of the humans are truly one.

In the world of the patriarchs, too, God is still very much like a human character. He enters and leaves the stage, approaches people and engages in conversation with them without special notice, in a matter-of-fact style. No cloud of smoke is necessary, no extraordinary light phenomena, or burying your face between your knees. The coming of the God of Abraham, Isaac, and Jacob is no news, and if he needs people to know his will, he will tell them in person. It is only with Moses that changes crawl in. The God he meets is much more than ever before "a fearful and fascinating mystery," to quote Rudolf Otto's classic definition of the holy. The revelations of this God are mystical and exceptional, and no ordinary person may know what he truly looks like: "no one shall see me and live" (Exod 33:20).

The hidden God reveals himself by hiding, in a burning bush, in a pillar of cloud or a pillar of fire, inside the curtain of the tent of meeting, or on a cloud-covered mountaintop with thunder and lightning and the blast of a trumpet. Moses alone may know him, even though he cannot know God's essence, his full nature; so it is his lot to act as a mediator between God and his people.

Assisted by Moses, God makes the necessary preparations for his departure to heaven. He wants to make sure he will be remembered when he is gone, and he insists that each generation will be reminded of him:

> When your children ask you in time to come, "What is the meaning of the decrees and the statutes and the ordinances that the Lord our God has commanded you?" then you shall say to your children, "We were Pharaoh's slaves in Egypt, but the Lord brought us out of Egypt with a mighty hand. The Lord displayed before our eyes great and awesome signs and wonders against Egypt, against Pharaoh and all his household. He brought us out from there in order to bring us in, to give us the land that he promised on oath to our ancestors. Then the Lord commanded us to observe all these statutes, to fear the Lord our God, for our lasting good, so as to keep us alive, as is now the case. If we diligently observe this entire commandment before the Lord our God, as he has commanded us, we will be in the right." (Deut 6:20–25)

Israel's rescue from Egypt is something to remember. Yet it is the law that enables God to retire from service, when his people embark on a new life in the promised land. From now on the law is the medium of God's presence. Its directions guide people to responsible living now that God himself is no longer there to give personal advice. And indeed,

> Never since has there arisen a prophet in Israel like Moses, whom the LORD knew face to face. (Deut 34:10)

Once the Torah, the law of Moses, established itself as the supreme authority of the Jewish religion, there was no way God could come back. The

Talmud tells the story (reported entertainingly by Visotzky in *Reading the Book*) of a Rabbi Joshua, who refused to take into account a voice from heaven in a debate of the law. The point he made was that the law "is not in heaven" (Deut 30:12). Since God has tasked his people to observe it, he has no right to intervene in its interpretation. Upon hearing Rabbi Joshua's words, God smiled and said, "My children have outwitted me."

Separation Anxiety

According to traditional Jewish thinking, God's prophetic Spirit has left the world for good. In the time of the patriarchs, all righteous people had it. When the Israelites fell to idolatry and worshipped the golden calf, it was limited to a few: prophets, high priests, and kings. With the death of the last writing prophets, Haggai, Zechariah, and Malachi, it was quenched altogether, due to the sins of the people. Since then, the best you could hope to hear was a remote echo of God's voice from heaven, a poor substitute, as the story of Rabbi Joshua so aptly illustrates.

In the New Testament, however, the Spirit makes a flamboyant return. It descends like a dove from heaven on Jesus in his baptism. After all these years, God is here again, truly in the flesh, as John the Evangelist is so keen to emphasize.

Yet he is not here to stay, not even this time. The Gospels are stories of bereavement, with the community of Jesus' followers in the leading role. The believers will need to grow stronger and more independent, so that they may survive after Jesus has returned to his Father in heaven.

It is the disciples who represent the community in the narrative. Each evangelist has his own take on their character. In Mark's gospel, they are outstandingly obdurate, whereas in John they fail to understand the metaphoric, spiritual meaning of Jesus' words. Yet in all four Gospels the story line again bears the marks of a coming-of-age story.

First, the disciples leave everything familiar behind. They have an intoxicating taste of power and freedom, as they pluck heads of grain despite the Sabbath law and eat without washing their hands, against the tradition of the elders. They rebel against authorities and dream of future accomplishments, high-ranking positions, and seats of honor at the service of God's kingdom. They gain a foretaste of these, as Jesus sends them out to proclaim the good news and heal the sick.

Yet this carefree apostolic youth will not last forever. Soon the disciples will learn that Jesus will not always be there for them, even if they should need his guidance. This presents a problem, as the disciples have no one else to go to. They have left house and occupation, wealth and source of income, the support of their families, and the trust of the authorities. If they wish to survive, they must learn to make it on their own. This will take place through trials and hardships. The greatest obstacles, it turns out, are their own fear and selfishness.

In the Gospels, fear is the opposite of faith. While faith enables action, fear brings it to a halt. The challenges are admittedly daunting: to feed thousands of people in a barren desert; to keep calm in a tiny boat in a raging sea storm; to walk on the water without sinking. The disciples fail. Evidently, they must change and grow.

It is not only their attitudes but also their values that need repair. The disciples argue with one another who is the greatest and shoo away people who bring little children to Jesus. Surely their master will not waste his time on minors! Time and again, Jesus has to explain to them that God's rule will establish a different order: whoever wants to be first must be the servant of all. Power means responsibility for the well-being of others. Sometimes this may even involve giving your own life so that others may live.

Renouncing yourself is the true source of that freedom that the disciples so desperately crave. Wealth and weapons bring no peace of mind; as long as you put your trust in them, you will never be free. Like faith, freedom requires that you overcome fear and learn to live with vulnerability.

Close to the end of story, it still looks like the disciples are going to fail miserably. Judas betrays Jesus, and Jesus is taken away for execution. The other disciples give in to their fear and flee. Peter, their leader, holds on for a while but eventually ends up denying Jesus three times.

Unlike in a modern coming-of-age story, the disciples will not learn their lesson all by themselves. Salvation is not from humanity but from God. It is only after the disciples meet the risen Christ and receive the Holy Spirit that they can see the world in a different light. Then it is time for Jesus to return to his Father in heaven. The disciples are finally ready to be incorporated in a new community that will bear their name—the apostolic church.

There was real demand for a story like the Gospels, because Jesus' long-term departure was not readily accepted by everyone. The first generation of Christians believed he would be back very soon. After all, it was such a long time since God's last visit on earth. Did he really have to leave so early?

Even later, Christians have never been quite as happy with their selection of stand ins for God's presence as Rabbi Joshua was with the law. The idea of an apocalyptic God who intrudes in human reality continues to be cherished even among those Christians who do not anticipate Jesus' immediate return. The Holy Spirit is not only "another Advocate" (John 14:16) sent by the Father to replace Jesus, but also "the Spirit of the Lord" who communicates Jesus' real presence in his church. Major denominations like the Roman Catholics, Episcopalians, and Lutherans believe Jesus is materially present in the Eucharist. And while Judaism and Islam categorically deny that human art can depict the divine, Christian artists have for centuries striven to open a window into what no eye has seen.

Popular Heroes

The heroes of the Hebrew Bible—patriarchs and kings—lend themselves well to patterns of personal growth. Yet originally, they featured as symbols of a collective, national identity. Their stories were about an entire community's coming-of-age.

Jesus' disciples, on the other hand, are in many ways models for the individual reader. Sometimes they function as paragons of faith the reader is expected to emulate. Perhaps more often, however, the reader is to learn from their mistakes. Much of the advice Jesus gives to his disciples applies to the original (and every so often, contemporary) audience as well. Jesus is thus speaking to two audiences at the same time, one within the narrative and another outside of it: "What I say to you I say to all" (Mark 13:37).

It is fascinating what sort of people the evangelists put up as exemplary and with whom they thought their audience would identify. For the most part, the Gospels bristle with ordinary folks: peasants and tax collectors, servant girls, and little children. Jesus' followers were a popular movement portrayed with a touch of realism. Herein, too—and this is another point Erich Auerbach makes in *Mimesis*—the Bible moves away from the requirements of classical style. In classical antiquity, the representation of common, everyday reality properly belonged to comedy. Heroes were not made at random. Nobility only occurred among the nobles, and it had to be depicted in high style. The sorrows of an aristocrat, presented with appropriate skill, were readily perceived as tragic. The blunderings of the poor, on the other hand, were considered laughable and had their place in pieces written for amusement.

Not so in the Gospels. The early Christian narrative transcends the limits of the ancient, classical representation of reality in a way that corresponds to modern realism's takeoff from classicism at the beginning of the nineteenth century. Auerbach takes as an example the story of Peter's denial according to the Gospel of Mark:

> They took Jesus to the high priest; and all the chief priests, the elders, and the scribes were assembled. Peter had followed him at a distance, right into the courtyard of the high priest; and he was sitting with the guards, warming himself at the fire. (Mark 14:53–54)

> While Peter was below in the courtyard, one of the servant girls of the high priest came by. When she saw Peter warming himself, she stared at him and said, "You also were with Jesus, the man from Nazareth." But he denied it, saying, "I do not know or understand what you are talking about." And he went out into the forecourt. Then the cock crowed. And the servant girl, on seeing him, began again to say to the bystanders, "This man is one of them." But again he denied it. Then after a little while the bystanders again said to Peter, "Certainly you are one of them; for you are a Galilean." But he began to curse, and he swore an oath, "I do not know this man you are talking about." At that moment the cock crowed for the second time. Then Peter remembered that Jesus had said to him, "Before the cock crows twice, you will deny me three times." And he broke down and wept. (Mark 14:66–72)

This is a noble and tragic story, yet it takes place down "below in the courtyard," among a group of servants, while the council and the guards are abusing Jesus in the palace of the high priest. Ordinary people engage in brief, direct dialogues in common language. Drawing on popular traditions, the narrative follows no particular style as would be required by its theme and topic.

Why isn't Peter a comic character? Because the Gospels break down the difference between the levels of high and low style, so that the tragic and the noble mix with the crude and the common. Indifferent to social convention, the Christian God finds home among lower-class people. Dying a scornful, ridiculed death, he comes to transform tragedy forever.

This beneficial mixing of styles was not so much a deliberate artistic program as a sign of the times and a corollary of the characteristics of Christianity as a socioreligious movement. The Gospels show, by the standards of their time, only a little literary ambition or skill. Their realism (quite like the realism of the early nineteenth-century writers, too) was a result of a particular historical need: suddenly, it became necessary to depict a world not of a stable and unchanging state of order, but invaded by fundamental transformations that concerned everybody, or anyone: "So if anyone is in Christ, there is a new creation: everything old has passed away; see, everything has become new!" (2 Cor 5:17). This reality could not be grasped by following classicist rules of style. This was because those rules made sense of the world by adjusting human experience to fixed categories, moral and artistic. In the impending revaluation of all values, those categories had not much to offer. The new wine would burst the old wineskins.

Biblical characters are determined by two fundamental questions: how will the divine fit in this mundane world, and how will its presence, immediate or mediated, transform human life? There is no definitive answer. On the one hand, humans are portrayed as dependent on God, who knows how much more there is in their heart than their words and actions can ever imply. On the other hand, growth means independence and takes humanity into a world where God is present no more, except in memory. Herein the Bible is not far from psychoanalytic theory: every baby is eventually weaned; we all must give up the illusion of unconstrained satisfaction and face reality as it is, indifferent to our needs and demands. Presence is replaced by desire, limitless fulfillment by the limited good.

Or is it? Aren't religion, art, and play the exclusive areas of human life wherein the battle between dreams and reality remains inconclusive? Even if God was happy to move away to heaven, his children might not let go of him that easily. They would rather continue to meet him in the word of the Scriptures, substance of the sacraments, prayer of the heart, and life devoted to justice. Is this good or bad, denial of reality or openness to imagination? Is religion a hindrance to personal growth, or a pathway to it?

5

A Malady or a Cure?

Is Faith Good for You?

There is a fine line between true religion and wishful fantasy. According to the Letter to the Hebrews, "faith is the assurance of things hoped for, the conviction of things not seen" (Heb 11:1). Believers are dissidents towards common reality. They will not bow to the obvious, and they reserve the right to rely on other things than mere cold facts—even if this means being criticized for foolishness. Listen to Paul speak to the church in Corinth:

> But God chose what is foolish in the world to shame the wise; God chose what is weak in the world to shame the strong; God chose what is low and despised in the world, things that are not, to reduce to nothing things that are. (1 Cor 1:27–28)

Paul's words contain remarkable subversive potential. Who decides by what standards individual people are to be considered wise or powerful or noble anyway? Sometimes reality, and social reality in particular, deserves to be challenged. This is one reason why there is demand for the kind of idealism that is the business of religion.

On the other hand, common reality has found strong supporters, too. They have accused religion of deliberate or instinctive self-deception. Karl Marx famously called it the opium of the people. The dream of a better world is a convenient painkiller: it helps the poor and the oppressed to put up with their lot.

Likewise, Sigmund Freud suggested that religion is based on denial. Faith feeds an infantile fantasy that all good deeds will be duly rewarded, life has a meaning beyond itself, and death will not be the end. Religious myths and rituals correspond to obsessive thinking and behavior that are meant to repress unpleasant truths. No psychologically mature persons need religion, as they will be able to face reality as it is. They will be perfectly happy with virtue as its own reward, life as meaning in itself, and death as its natural and complete ending.

Although Freud later adjusted his critical stance towards religion, many of his followers remained skeptical. Only in recent years has a different psychoanalysis of religion gained strength, emphasizing the positive role of religion as a means to cope with reality and provide it with meaning. Still, psychologists are known to be the least religious of all scientists (although this is perhaps for reasons more closely related to the equally long-standing tradition of empiricist, experimental psychology than that of Freudian psychoanalysis).

From time to time, psychological critics of religion have turned their critical eye on the Bible, too, to find support for their view of religion as harmful. As a rule, they have found biblical characters delusional, narcissistic, megalomaniac, or just out of balance in some way or another. In the late nineteenth and early twentieth centuries, there appeared a number of "pathographies" of Jesus, probing the four Gospels for psychopathological symptoms known to modern medical science. Many of those studies were triggered by Albert Schweitzer and Johannes Weiss's groundbreaking research on the historical figure of Jesus. In Schweitzer and Weiss's analysis, Jesus appeared not as the teacher of timeless truths he was widely thought to be at the time, but as a savage prophet of impending doom.

It seems that Schweitzer suffered from a bad conscience about people jumping to conclusions from his work. Perhaps this was why he, having changed careers from theology to medicine, chose contemporary psychiatric studies of Jesus as the topic of his research. In his doctoral dissertation he was able to demonstrate that those studies suffered from serious weaknesses—most of all, lack of source criticism and poor knowledge of the history of religion. Authors such as George de Loosten, William Hirsch, and Charles Binet-Sanglé had taken biblical accounts at face value, as if the Gospels were neutral and accurate reports of historical facts. In reality, however, the material these scholars drew on was mostly without any direct historical source value. As Schweitzer knew and mainstream biblical scholarship today agrees, many of Jesus' sayings about his divine nature and mission are best understood as dramatic commentary introduced by later editors, based on their christological beliefs. This being the case, one can hardly take those sayings as medical evidence of Jesus' mental state.

Nor were apocalyptic visions or the anticipation of imminent divine intervention singular products of Jesus' vivid imagination. Rather, they were a major element of the Judaism of his day. Shortly before Jesus, John the Baptist had been calling on people to repent in the face of coming judgment. Soon afterwards, Paul would be equally certain that the world was about to end during his lifetime. Austere prophets, wannabe Messiahs, and esoteric literature were the order of the day.

Add to this that turn-of-the-century psychiatric studies of Jesus took frequent recourse to novel, hypothetical syndromes unknown to the history of medicine, and it comes as little surprise that Schweitzer would rate them as "exactly zero" on both medical and historical grounds.[1] The only symptoms Jesus actually seemed to have had were his high self-esteem and, possibly, a vision he had on the occasion of his baptism. These were hardly enough to declare him insane. Rather, he seems to have been a more-or-less normal Jewish man in relatively good health.

What Is Wrong with Ezekiel?

Diagnoses of Jesus as mentally ill seem not to hold water. Might there be other characters in the Bible who actually did suffer from mental health problems?

Of all the biblical personalities, it must be Ezekiel, the exiled prophet, who appeared to need therapy the most. His behavior in the book that bears his name is nothing short of bizarre.

The book of Ezekiel originated in a situation where Jerusalem was conquered, its temple destroyed, and the political elite forcibly removed to live in Babylon. It was there that the prophet had his visions of God explaining what had happened and why, and how to move forward. Since then, generations of readers have been perplexed by Ezekiel's surrealistic inaugural vision (1:1–28) and the odd symbolic actions by means of which he communicated God's judgment to his people (4–5, 12). These included lying motionless on his side for over a year and baking his bread on human excrement, just to give two examples.

1. Schweitzer, *The Psychiatric Study of Jesus*, 73.

And there were more disturbing things to come. Chapters 16 and 23 are best described as pornographic. Portrayed as God's maiden brides, young Jerusalem and her sister Samaria have nymphomaniac sex with foreign nations and their patron gods. Repelled by this outrage, God their father gives them what is due: the destruction of these cities at the hand of the enemy was an appropriate punishment for their fall into idolatry. In Ezekiel's imagery, Jerusalem is not only God's bride but also his daughter, a foundling whom God adopted and raised to full womanhood, to be his queen. The narration is fraught with sadism and incest. It is no surprise that in the first century CE, the distinguished Rabbi Eliezer banned Ezekiel 16 from being read aloud in the synagogue.

Nor is it surprising that many modern scholars have resorted to medical explanations. Putting the prophet on the couch, they have asked what sort of personal problems, endogenous or arising from early childhood experiences, might have resulted in such a strange vision of the world.

In a recent doctoral dissertation, David G. Garber Jr. has documented the long history of diagnosing Ezekiel. It is impressive, to say the least. There is hardly a known disorder that has not been suggested as the cause of the prophet's condition. Catalepsy, for example, would match his periods of muteness and immobility, and do his symbolic actions not seem convulsive? Some believed he suffered from acute paranoid schizophrenia, manifested in symptoms such as catatonia, paranoid imagination, narcissistic-masochistic conflict with attendant fantasies of castration and sexual regression, schizophrenic withdrawal, and delusions of grandeur. Others proposed that his pathological misogyny originated in childhood abuse. The most recent studies have suggested that his strange behavior might have been caused by post-traumatic stress disorder. Rather than lost childhood experiences it would have been the more immediate experiences of war, the destruction of Jerusalem, and exile that traumatized him.

Yet Schweitzer's critical points on diagnosing Jesus hold true of Ezekiel as well. Psychiatric treatises on the prophet have received heavy criticism both from the guild of biblical scholarship and from the field of medical science. From a clinical point of view, psychiatric evaluation without in-depth interview or testing sounds questionable. A proper textual analysis, on the other hand, would require diligent source criticism and knowledge of the text's original context. Do all the accounts we have in the present book of Ezekiel originate in the same source? How reliable are they? How would they have been understood by the original audience? How much has the character of Ezekiel, as portrayed in the text, in common with any historical person? Could he be a traditional figure, or is he a symbolic representative of a tormented nation?

The heart of the problem is that the real analysand is not a person at all but a literary text. We would therefore do well to shift our attention from the supposed life history of an ancient prophet to the literary features of the document at hand. This is Garber's point; in his analysis, Ezekiel is a typical case of *literature of survival*. Works of this particular genre are produced and preserved in communities that suffered shocking, traumatic events. Characteristically, the literary structure of such works—the way they labor to describe and give meaning to a painful past—is suggestive of the dynamics of psychic trauma.

According to psychoanalytic thinking, psychic trauma is characterized by the psyche's compulsive attempt to summon up the memory of the traumatic experience in such a form that would make sense out of it. This is impossible, however, because traumatic experiences are by definition incomprehensible. While their impact cannot be erased, they can never be truly owned or embraced. They are simply more than we can take. What results is a "missed encounter," a mismatch of the event, its memory, and its meaning, as the hopeless attempt to make sense of the original experience results in its being repeated endlessly in an altered form in nightmares, hallucinations, dreams, compulsive thoughts and actions, in numbing or hypersensitivity.

By the same token, artistic representations of traumatic experiences are bound to be problematic. How can one relate the ineffable? This question has been raised in connection with the Jewish holocaust in particular, as all accounts of life in the Nazi death camp seem to miss its actual meaning as experienced by those who were part of it.

A traumatic history is something that cannot be fully understood. However it is approached or represented, it must be, as the Cornell critic Cathy Caruth puts it, *in replacement of understanding*. Stories of survival do not so much report past events, as they bear witness to their effect by making the audience encounter an eerie absence of comprehensible meaning. What results is an impression of strangeness: someone is speaking of the unspeakable.

Trauma renders language useless. Prosaic style is to no avail; a blunt, detached account would sound banal and cynical. Poetic language is of no more help: artistic play on a catastrophe would border on the hysterical. The only option left is a quasi-religious language characterized by ambiguity, multiple meanings, repetition, and what Terrence des Pres called a sense of "ultimate concern."[2] Realistic narration is replaced by vagueness, symbolism, and a frenzied attempt to convey meanings that cannot be articulated.

This, of course, is exactly what happens in the book of Ezekiel. Whether or not there ever was a historical prophet by that name, the biblical narrative seems to be haunted by a compulsion to tell what cannot be told. In this respect, it is a typical representative of the literature of survival. Time and again it attempts to make sense of the painful experiences of destruction and exile, and time and again these attempts take it beyond the boundaries of mimetic language to an idiosyncratic world of visions and parables. The end result, the traumatic history of a confounded people, so cruelly punished by their God for their infidelities, testifies to the original experience by signaling its absence.

As evidenced by the survival of Ezekiel in the Hebrew Bible, the book is essentially about a community. The loss it seeks to articulate affected the people collectively, and the same is true of the feelings of guilt and self-disgust that pervade it. The survivors shared a common need to encounter and cope with the past. This is why they saw to it that the text became a book and was preserved in their canon, no matter how odd or perverted it may have seemed in their eyes—or perhaps it was precisely because of that oddness that it became so important for them, as they realized this was as close as they could get to recovering the original, traumatic experience.

Crises and Grief Work

There may not be another book in the Bible so deeply traumatized as Ezekiel. Yet experiences of crises, dealing with them and getting over them, are at the very heart of the biblical narrative. The biblical story line rambles from one major crisis to another. The expulsion from paradise is no small loss, and the end of the world and the Last Judgment sound critical enough. Between these two cosmic megacrises there are plenty of minor catastrophes: the flood, the slavery in Egypt, the destruction of Jerusalem, the Babylonian captivity, the scandal of Jesus' death, the failure of the Christian mission among the Jews, and Jesus' delayed return. At the individual level, too, the biblical characters go through tribulations that put their faith to the test. The patriarchs must leave home for an unknown destination. Jesus'

2. As quoted in Garber, "Traumatizing Ezekiel."

followers are to leave house, wife, brothers, parents, and children for the sake of God's kingdom. The identity of the biblical God takes form through a series of crisis narratives. He is the one who hears cries for help, comes over, gives consolation, helps us through, restores hope, and encourages action.

But what sort of a counselor, or therapist, will a Savior God make? Will he lead people to acceptance, or is he rather encouraging a futile, unrealistic hope? How does biblical religion translate into our current language of mental health and well-being?

The Princeton theologian Donald Capps has sought to reconceive the role of the Bible in modern pastoral counseling. How might the Bible influence, for example, the way people today recover from grief or prepare for marriage? Issues of salvation and general morality aside, does the Good Book have anything in particular to say about the turning points of contemporary life? If it has, would that differ from, support, or add value to what psychotherapies, life coaches, and self-help books can offer? And, for the purposes of our present discussion, would that represent healthy realism or harmful denial?

The answer is everything but self-evident. There is often little difference between professional pastoral care, as conducted in mainline churches, and standard crisis or family therapy, even if the former is somehow informed by an indistinct Christian ethos. Moreover, many pastoral theologians have grown wary of bringing the Bible to bear in their work, and for what seem to be good reasons: the ancient text does not lend itself well to a handbook for counseling, nor can all its advice be recommended just as it is. In fact, many known examples of "biblical counseling" are discomforting from a modern point of view: some recommend corporal punishment of children (a criminal offense in my country), others the submission of wives to their husbands (something many people would consider extremely primitive).

Capps takes a very different approach. He makes use of results gained from critical, academic studies of the Bible. In biblical literature as well as elsewhere certain literary and traditional genres are designed for certain purposes. The structure of a didactic speech, for example, differs from that of an obituary or a sonnet, because each of them works by different means to a different end. So, if you compare, say, a number of biblical accounts of Jesus' healings, you will soon discover a pattern that repeats itself. Standard features combine to make the story memorable and easy to follow, to create suspense, to emphasize the extraordinary nature of the event and the key role faith had in making it all happen.

First, there is an appeal for help, made by the sick person or his or her auxiliary. Then, an obstacle occurs, such as a dense crowd blocking the way to Jesus. Once the obstacle is overcome, we are told how the persons recovered exactly as Jesus said they would. Jesus then commends the persons for their faith, sends them away, and insists that they tell no one what happened. Finally, the narrative concludes with the reaction of the audience: the crowd is amazed, while Jesus' enemies start to plot against him.

Capps's point is that now, as before, biblical texts are best suited for their original purpose. Sometimes that purpose is recovery from loss (as in psalms of lament), sometimes it is that we recognize the consequences of our actions (as in Proverbs) or suddenly see our lives in a different light (as in the parables of Jesus). The therapeutic qualities of texts are in their structures as much as in their contents—which is good, because even if the content should be dated or context-bound, the form may still work as a basis for new applications.

Drawing on Walter Brueggeman's work on the biblical psalms of lament, Capps makes an informative structural comparison between the lament and Elisabeth Kübler-Ross's well-known five-stage model of grief work. The two have marked similarities. They both provide a structure for recovery from a personal or communal loss. They also allow expression of anger. However, whereas the Kübler-Ross model's fifth and final stage is open-ended—acceptance may stand for resignation or reconciliation—the typical lament concludes with a happy ending: the supplicant becomes assured that God will help.

Psalm of Lament	*Stages of Grief Work (Kübler-Ross)*
Address to God	Denial and Isolation
Complaint	Anger
Confession of Trust	Bargaining
Petition	Depression
Words of Assurance	Acceptance
Vow to Praise	

Perhaps the psalm should make no promises? Does an over-optimistic reliance on divine intervention not border on denial? This is certainly an option the lament, and all religion, make available. We may choose to use it as a source of comforting illusions, and leave it at that. Yet this is hardly all religious traditions can offer, and it would be inaccurate to see escapism as their conclusive answer to people in distress. Drawing on centuries of experience in crisis recovery, they should fare better.

And indeed, on a closer look, the lament, too, bears closer resemblance to a solution-focused talking cure than to a mere comforting illusion summoned up to evade grief. First, in the course of the lament all sorts of feelings are freely spoken out, in a clearly recognizable form: fear, anger, resentment, even paranoia. The supplicant will meet his or her personal demons out in the open. Second, the actual content of the petition—what the supplicant ends up asking for—makes a great difference. At its most primitive, petition remains bargaining, bent to denial: can we please agree that God wipe away my disease, my enemies, all my past miseries as if they never existed? In a more developed form, however, the petition can help articulate what one needs the most to live on: courage; strength to endure the longing; confidence that one can make it, even without what has been lost. Some individual psalms come up with more realism than others.

From the perspective of realism, the most critical part of the lament is no doubt its ending, where the supplicant praises God for hearing all prayers. Not only do we receive the good at the hand of God, but also the bad. This gives poor support to any ideal image of God as a guardian of happy endings. This conflict has obviously made itself felt, since the history of psalmic literature displays a discernible development towards greater realism. In the books of Isaiah, Hosea, and Jeremiah, a new version of the lament emerges. In *God's lament*, God himself bemoans the afflictions he must bring on his people due to their transgressions. This is a major turning point in biblical literature. The God of realism catches up with the God of fantasy. The intervening God, who used to reward the faithful with oxen and sheep and slay the wicked with famine and plague, is joined by and gradually gives way to a compassionate God, a source of hope rather than retaliation. While the compassionate God will not necessarily step in and rescue his servant from "the arrow that flies by day, or the pestilence that stalks in darkness" (Ps 91:5–6), he will pity the desolate and "weep with those who weep" (Rom 12:15).

Later on, the compassionate God will grow more prominent. In the Christian Bible, he goes so far as to leave his heavenly abode and become a human among others, to share human pain and vulnerability:

> ... though he was in the form of God,
> [he] did not regard equality with God
> as something to be exploited,
> but emptied himself,
> taking the form of a slave,
> being born in human likeness.
> And being found in human form,
> he humbled himself
> and became obedient to the point of death—
> even death on a cross.
> (Phil 2:6–8)

It is true that he will later resume his power in full:

> Therefore God also highly exalted him
> and gave him the name
> that is above every name,
> so that at the name of Jesus
> every knee should bend,
> in heaven and on earth and under the earth,
> and every tongue should confess
> that Jesus Christ is Lord,
> to the glory of God the Father.
> (Phil 2:9–11)

But this would only take place at the end of days, at the Last Judgment, or in eternity. Meanwhile, neither the Father nor the Son will walk the earth to see that evildoers be punished and enemies destroyed. Instead, the compassionate God will make the sun rise on the evil and the good, and send rain both on the godly and the wicked.

So, traveling with humans seems to have refined God's character: the trigger-happy world policeman has grown into a keen listener. The original promise of a timely and decisive intervention on behalf of the righteous has lost credibility, as injustice, unfairness, and misery abound in the world. At the same time, however, the claim that God understands what people go through and feels sympathy for them gains new weight. Great wonders are replaced with silent appreciation and assurance of worth: no matter how life may treat people, they are still of immense value to God, more so than sparrows, ravens, or lilies, which are not insignificant, either (cf. Matt 6:25–34; 10:29–31; Luke 12:6–7, 22–31).

In a sense, the compassionate God has paid the price of becoming more real. He is considerably smaller than the old intervening God was. Yet he has the advantage of being commensurate with the present reality and therefore not being rejected by it. He has grown to accept, for the time being, the reality he is said to have created, and reality is willing to tolerate him in return, as a matter of faith.

As in the development of a human individual, a sense of reality and a sense of being separate go together. Just as a little child gradually comes to understand that the outside world is there quite independently, so the believer should see that God is not pulling the strings of the universe just to make some individual people happy or miserable. Unalleviated suffering or overwhelming joy is not a sign of God's anger or favor, but part of the human condition. Not getting your way does not mean that nobody cares.

A Good-Enough God

The New Testament story of Jesus repeats the story of God's coming-of-age and brings it to conclusion. The fantasy of having God here with us, dispelling all evil for good, is transformed into a longing for a caring God, a tolerance for his absence and for the world's inevitable imperfections.

It all starts with a dream come true. Jesus heals the sick, raises dead, and preaches the good news to the poor. He appears as a source of endless well-being, satisfying people's needs and making them whole, so that they will want no more: "Whoever comes to me will never be hungry, and whoever believes in me will never be thirsty" (John 6:35).

Soon it will turn out, however, that following Jesus is no key to happiness. The road to life is narrow and goes through the narrow gate. There is no resurrection without suffering and death. This is a difficult lesson for Jesus' disciples to learn, as they are quite fond of their original fantasy of personal success. They keep dreaming of power, no matter how ardently Jesus tries to wean them from it. They argue with one another as to who is the greatest and engage in rivalry for prominent positions in the coming kingdom of God. This claim to power, comfort, and security, however, is precisely what they need to abandon. Jesus' followers are not to lord it over other people, but rather to be slaves of all. This makes them vulnerable to persecution, suffering, and death. Jesus himself is destined to suffer at the hands of his enemies.

The news about the necessity of suffering traumatizes the disciples, and they will not take in the message. Peter rebukes Jesus directly: "God forbid it, Lord! This must never happen to you" (Matt 16:22). Yet reality rushes in, over and over again. Jesus' words repeat themselves like a traumatic memory. On the road to Jerusalem he predicts his passion and death three times.

The story that began as a clean-cut fantasy is gradually transformed into a story about the necessity of a loss. The disciples witness the Almighty Son of God being wounded and dying, to go away and turn into symbols. Feeding miracles will be replaced by the bread and the wine of the Eucharist, and Jesus' care for his own survives in their own capacity to love: "love one another as I have loved you" (John 15:12). The illusion of fulfilment in the present gives way to a longing for what once was and for what has not yet arrived. Utopia is turned into action, directed by ideals, yet conditioned by reality.

So, the moral of the gospel story is actually not that far from Freud's ideal of being at ease with the limitations of human life. In fact, it is quite in line with what some psychoanalysts view as the human predicament of clinging to the "perfect good." According to Melanie Klein and contemporary Kleinian theory, and the British object relations theorists, such as W. R. D. Fairbairn and D. W. Winnicott, the little child initially takes the mother's presence for granted: the mother and the child are one, so that the mother will immediately provide whatever care the child may want. Soon, however, the child must give up this illusion of endless gratification and come to terms with the outside world. This requires an ability to tolerate ambiguity. The child needs to understand that both pleasure and pain originate in one and the same reality. At first, the child cannot do this. Instead, it splits its experience of the world in two: the "good mother" who offers gratification and the "bad mother" who causes frustration are two different things. Thus the child protects the image of the "good mother" as well as the image of a "good me." To keep the "good mother" safe and intact, the child introjects its negative experiences of the mother inwards: that is not mummy; this is my fault. On the other hand, the child externalizes its innate aggressiveness and projects it onto the "bad mother." This results in a fantasy of persecution: it is not me; the "bad mother" wants to hurt me.

The more care and nurture the child receives, the faster and better it learns to tolerate both frustration and its own destructiveness, and the less need there is to protect the "good mother" and "good self" by means of splitting. As soon as the child understands that negative feelings will not devour the good in the world, the impeccable "good mother" is replaced by a more realistic image of a "good-enough mother" who needs not be flawless in order to be safe.

Yet the tendency to split remains in us all throughout our lives. In states of strong psychic conflict, severe pressure, passionate love, or religious fervor, we are inclined to protect our love objects by forming idealized images of them. Thus we regard them as pure and flawless, incapable of causing negative feelings of any kind. Should such negative feelings arise, we either project them onto others (each onto our favorite enemy), or introject them back into us, blaming ourselves for not being worthy of the good things we have. This kind of behavior is known to take place on a group level, too. For political or religious extremists, the absolute perfection of their own group, its leaders, and their ideology is something they will not contest. Whatever frustration it may make them feel, they transform that feeling into guilt or develop a paranoia to explain why they should feel worried. Whoever is with them is with the children of light; those who oppose them are already condemned.

It is for this very reason that God's gradual departure from the biblical narrative is so important and his becoming one of us vulnerable men and women so meaningful. Like a caring parent, God transforms from pure excellence into good enough. Instead of shielding his children from all the evils of the world and making them dependent on his perfection, he prepares them for adulthood and supports their ability to not take hardships personally. It is the same Jesus who both proclaims salvation to all people and prepares them for suffering. Not only does he raise the dead; he is also about to share their fate. The Risen One bears the marks of crucifixion on his body: not even God himself can visit the human condition and remain unharmed.

In an ideal world, the story of God and humanity might eventually end up on a secure path towards mature spirituality. In reality, however, life tends to be more complicated. Rather than steady growth, life is a constant struggle between the desires of the heart and the demands of reality. So God, too, is not prone to staying put in heaven but tends to return among people when a form of religious practice makes that possible. This is what happens when the followers of Jesus (or Mahdi, or some other departed-yet-expected-to-return Savior) become convinced that his second coming is at hand and the longing for his presence transmutes into a certainty of being one with him already. Again, the same takes place when some sacred place, writing, or spiritual leader becomes divine in the devotees' eyes. To remain so, it must be kept pure—so that any sign of deficiency must be split from it and removed to somewhere else, typically to a person or a group of people suitable for scapegoating. Someone must be sacrificed so that the dream of the many may come true.

While psychological splitting is not healthy, it is found everywhere where there is religion. In a sense, dealing with God is risky: his maturity can only come after his childhood; in order to leave this world, he must first reveal himself there—and once he has shown himself capable of doing that, he can easily call again. When he first left his heavenly abode, he tore an irreparable rift in the fabric separating his realm from ours. Since the discovery of God, heaven and earth have never been quite separate again.

Perhaps this is good. An absolutely airtight reality with no way for any inappropriate fantasy to enter might prove fatal to our dreams and ideals. Like erotic love, the desire for God is powered by a dream of a seamless union, an ultimate satisfaction that is as impossible to renounce as it is to achieve. It would be like renouncing one's soul.

Growing Up

While God's being human may sound radical, the human nature of human beings should come as little surprise. God's excellence and our human limitations make a rather perfect couple.

Yet in the Bible God creates humankind in his image, so that the biblical image of God and the biblical image of humanity are closely interlinked. Likewise, in the history of biblical interpretation, divine perfection often sets a measure for humanity as well.

In traditional Christian interpretation, human beings were meant to be more like God. If all had gone well, humans would have remained immortal and morally flawless. In other words, what we now call being human—that is, corporeality, fallibility, and mortality—was not originally in human nature. Rather, it was a result of a cosmic misfortune, a fall from grace. Salvation, correspondingly, involves a return from our present human condition to a likeness of God.

From a human point of view, this is a tough equation: to do away with our humanity is at the same time a religious obligation and, due to our fallen state, categorically impossible. Although Christianity introduces God's grace as a patent solution, such an ideal raises questions. Does it mean that we are all born lacking and guilty, just for being what we are? How can anyone be responsible for something that is not in their power?

The Christian idea of the fall is based on the biblical story of paradise (Gen 2:4b—3:24). The prevailing interpretation reads the story as being about the fall of humanity into sin. The narrative would recount how sin and death became part of this world and humanity descended to its present state of moral fallibility, physical vulnerability, and finite existence. This was all our fault—God would have hoped otherwise.

The key question for interpretation is at which point of the story Adam and Eve—the first man and the first woman—are first to be identified as humans. If read as a story of the fall, the narrative would be about their losing their original humanity and becoming less than they actually are. Yet there is another reading to the story, one that sees the narrative as a *creation myth of humanity*. In this interpretation, Adam and Eve first become fully human only at the end of the narrative, as they become aware of their human condition, leave the womb of paradise, and step into reality. What took place before that was not a fall but development into responsible, independent human life.

The biblical scholar Lyn Bechtel reads the paradise story along these lines, as a myth of human maturation. She, too, finds comparison between the biblical narrative and developmental psychology useful and intriguing. In the story, Adam and Eve are properly named as the image of man and the mother of all life. True to human form, they begin their life like children: naked and feeling no shame. Their surroundings provide them with everything they may want: in the garden, every tree is pleasant to the sight and good for food.

The trees are also symbols of growth. Like people, they grow taller slowly, without notice. Their phallic-shaped trunks evoke associations with male sexuality and their ability to bear fruit to female sexuality. The way they shed their leaves in autumn and sprout anew in springtime testifies to the great cycle of life.

Among the trees of paradise, two have a special meaning. *The tree of life* represents the fantasy of eternal life, or childlike trust in endless, uninterrupted care and nurture. As long as the man and the woman remain in their original state of innocence, God will not forbid them to eat from this tree. Not knowing the complexity of life protects their journey toward adulthood. So that this illusion may continue, the children must not eat from *the tree of the knowledge of good and evil*. In the story (as well as in Near Eastern lore in general) the fruits of this tree are symbols of sexual awakening, moral consciousness, and experience of the world and the human condition. This is why to eat them is to know death: a rite of passage, it welcomes the initiate to the community of mortals.

Children lack the capacity for critical thinking. Therefore, the essence of morality for Adam and Eve, too, is obedience: they will do as they are told. It is only in adolescence that questioning and, indeed, disobedience, become appropriate and necessary, if one is to learn moral discernment. Meanwhile, Adam rehearses his social and language skills, first by giving names to different sorts of animals and then learning to know the woman, made of his rib. For the first time in the narrative we hear him speak.

On arrival at adolescence, obedience is no longer an adequate basis for personal choices. While children learn from their parents, the adolescent must engage with life itself and learn from experience. In the paradise story, experience crawls in with the snake. A symbol of wisdom and a stock mediating figure in ancient Near Eastern literature, the snake represents an understanding of the complexity of life (this is quite appropriate, as some snakes are poisonous and some are not).

So it becomes the task of the snake to lead the humans towards the knowledge of good and evil. The time has come for them to enter adulthood, open their eyes, and see the world as it really is. The woman goes first. As in real life, the female matures earlier than the male. The snake prompts her to give up her childish, concrete ways of thinking: death will not follow instantly upon eating of the tree of knowledge. The fruit—the key to alluring adult life—looks ideally beautiful to her. She eats, then gives some to her husband, and he eats, too.

Adult realities prove to be less than ideal. The man and the woman find themselves naked and exposed to feelings of vulnerability, defenselessness, inadequacy, and shame. These feelings hit them hard because their identity is not yet well formed. They look for shelter and cover themselves with leaves.

Enter God, and like the snake, he asks the couple a series of rhetorical questions. Recognizing their new status as adults, he now expects them to assume responsibility for their actions. This is all new to them, however, and they do their best to avoid it: he puts the blame on her, whereas she blames the deceitful snake.

Then God goes on to explain to them the potentials and limitations of adult life. The woman's sexuality and capacity to give birth make her God's partner in creation, yet they bring her pain and peril, too. As a sign of her newly acquired fertility she receives a new name: Eve, the mother of all life. Like the woman, the man, too, has an ambivalent relationship with nature. The earth will provide him with food to eat, but not without toil and labor. The man and the woman are thus introduced to the facts of life, the most severe of which is death. Man (Hebrew, *adam*) is dust (Hebrew, *adama*), and to dust he must return.

Finally, God prepares the couple for their journey from their childhood home. Having made them clothes and dressed them, he notes that they are now like him, knowing good and evil. He sees them off, hoping they will start a family and make a living. Then he seals off the gates of paradise and blocks the way to the tree of life for good. There is no return to the carefree days of childhood.

The way we choose to read the paradise story makes all the difference, because it will determine the biblical idea of humanity for us. In Bechtel's view, her developmental interpretation is not only correct in terms of history of religion; it is also the only reading that is morally sound. To think that the human condition was God's punishment for Adam and Eve's disobedience would be to idealize regression and induce guilt for what is part of normal human development into adulthood. Assuming a world like ours was part of God's plan, the loss of paradise was a pure necessity, an entrance fee to human life.

Like the golden days of childhood (for those of us who were so fortunate), the original paradisiacal fantasy will never fully fade away. In Judaism, Christianity, and Islam, paradise awaits the believers in the indeterminate future. Life is set between two identical fantasies and gains its meaning from them.

So, fantasy has its place. It only becomes risky if confused with reality. The crucial thing for the sense of reality is not that we replace our fantasies with realism but that we can tell them apart. The presence of fulfillment (the tree of life) and the presence of desire (the tree of knowledge) are mutually exclusive.

Both the ability to dream and the ability to give up our dreams for the sake of reality are essential for our well-being. A minimum amount of faith, hope, and love is necessary, so that we can enjoy our lives, make moral decisions, and build lasting relationships with other people. Cynicism and disillusionment devour joy and empathy. On the other hand, we must adjust our ideals to reality. A responsible person will compromise his or her personal desires for the greater good. Getting lost in fantasy is dangerous for the self as well as for others.

Religion involves a strong fantasy component. That is why it has been compared to sedatives, self-deceit, and even mental disorder. Yet religions are engaged in the same struggle between dreams and reality as every other aspect of human life. On the one hand, they open the way for otherworldly visions that have no place here on earth; yet without them, the world would go blind to its innermost hopes and desires. On the other hand, sound religion guards the gates of paradise and insists that faith and knowledge are two different things. The kingdom of heaven has not arrived, not here, not yet. Meanwhile, the world stays, and the never-ending desire for fulfilment keeps it on the move.

6

A Story without a Beginning

Do You Understand What You Are Reading?

What does an ideal reader of the Bible look like? The Bible itself provides us with some examples. In the Acts of the Apostles, chapter eight, an Ethiopian eunuch, an official of the Ethiopian royal court, is returning home from pilgrimage. Seated in his carriage, he is reading the prophet Isaiah. Philip the deacon comes across him on the road and asks him, "Do you understand what you are reading?" He replies, "How can I, unless someone guides me?" Philip then explains to him that the passage is actually a prophecy about Jesus. The Ethiopian is convinced, and Philip baptizes him into the Christian faith (Acts 8:26–40).

The Ethiopian is a fine example of a paradigmatic character typical of Luke's narrative. He sets up a standard for the reader to follow. In this particular case, the standard is a standard of reading. Somewhat surprisingly, this model reader's most salient characteristic is his inability to understand the text. The moral of the story is that the Scriptures are riddles only an informed reader can crack. The key to their meaning will only be provided by a competent interpretive community, the Christian church, whose membership is open to every understanding reader. Once the Ethiopian learns to read like a Christian, he has become a Christian.

So, the art of biblical interpretation is older than the Christian (or Hebrew) Bible itself. The history of the Bible and the history of biblical interpretation are not so much successive as parallel processes. Within the Christian canon, the New Testament presents a new reading of the law and the prophets. In the Hebrew Bible, younger writings build on older ones. Even the most ancient parts of the text draw on previous traditions.

Along with the biblical books emerged oral and written commentary. Jewish scribes developed the exegesis of the law of Moses into a distinct form of art, while apocalyptic communities like the Essenes—and Christians—kept record of biblical prophecies they believed had come true in their midst. At the time the Christian Bible reached its current composition, there had already been centuries of biblical interpretation.

The more ancient, the more widespread, and the more authoritative the text, the more it will be in need of interpretation. With every passing year, and with every cultural border crossed, understanding becomes ever-more difficult, yet it remains imperative that the text be understood fully and correctly. So, when the youngest of the biblical books were still in the making, generations of scribes had already put their best effort into untangling the oldest and the most revered parts of the holy writ. Their task was further complicated by the reticent style of the biblical authors: many a thing is left for the reader to infer.

In addition to adequate theological understanding, scriptural believers need practical applications. Changing circumstances create situations that the biblical authors could not possibly have anticipated. So the sage and the scribe are tasked, first, with finding the timeless core truth in the text, and then coming up with implications for current praxis. What is and is not appropriate behavior on the Sabbath day? When and how should I fast? Who is my neighbor? It is to questions like these that Jesus, the scribes of the Pharisees, and their sagacious colleagues have ever since been expected to provide answers.

The Written and the Spoken Word of God

Vital as it is, biblical exegesis can be an ungrateful trade. While the sanctity of biblical texts makes their correct interpretation crucial (and, typically, calls forth an entire professional community of commentators), there are still fears lest this violate their immaculate nature. Isn't the Bible the complete and unflawed word of God? Should it not be self-sufficient? What else is human judgment of God's word than inappropriate mistrust and contempt?

Different people have come up with different answers to these recurring worries. Jewish rabbis suggested that any interpretation of God's law is actually part of God's law, assuming it has been appropriately deduced from the biblical text. In other words, the text and its commentary are parts of one and the same revelation: besides *the written Torah*—that is, the five books of Moses—the law includes *the oral Torah*, the tradition of the elders on how the written Torah should be understood and put into practice. Moses received them both at Mount Sinai, yet while the written Torah was immediately accessible in its entirety ("very near you . . . for you to observe," cf. Deut 30:14), the oral Torah would only come into light gradually, as future generations became doers of the word in their own lives.

The oral Torah may have an infamous ring in the ears of some Christians. Isn't that the very kind of nitpicking that turns God's gracious will into trivial casuistry? Didn't Jesus himself rebuke the Pharisees for not seeing the forest for the trees:

> For you tithe mint, dill, and cumin, and have neglected the weightier matters of the law: justice and mercy and faith. It is these you ought to have practiced without neglecting the others. You blind guides! You strain out a gnat but swallow a camel! (Matt 23:23–24)

The Pharisees, of course, would have felt differently. For them, the entire law, gnats and all, was a unique blessing, a singular source of holiness on earth. It was their dream to bring that blessing to bear on every Jew, regardless of status, wealth, or occupation. The oral Torah made this possible. It provided an all-inclusive framework for applying priestly holiness to every area of life, including situations no one had experienced before.

As long as the temple stood in Jerusalem, the Pharisees were only one Jewish revivalist movement among many. However, when the Roman army destroyed the temple in the year 70, this created an all-new demand for the Pharisaic idea of quotidian holiness. How could the Jews keep observing the law now that the temple was gone? Surely there was no other way to perform all the rites and offerings that God had commanded, was there? Yes there was, the Pharisees would say: the Jewish community itself is the temple, and the Jewish way of life is an enduring holy service. This worked; rabbinic Judaism was built on the basis laid by the Pharisees.

The beauty of the oral Torah is that it grows endlessly with every new situation. New interpretations are deduced from previous ones, and there are as many kinds of interpretations as there are people. Some are tediously minute, others universally broad. One rabbi might say that you must not start your car on the Sabbath, because the Torah forbids making a fire on the day of rest and that applies to the spark plug, too. On the other hand, a particular statute may be taken to represent a universal principle. Leviticus, for example, advises not to put on a garment made of two different materials (Lev 19:19)—from which you might infer that matters of dissimilar nature (like religion and politics, or sports events and beer tents) mix badly in general.

The diversity of interpretations means that the oral Torah is all about discussion. Rabbinic literature is made of quotations: this rabbi said such and such, and that rabbi disagreed. In most cases, the disagreements are allowed to prevail. There is no vote; instead, everyone may choose whom they will follow, or they may present yet another interpretation, and meet the inevitable counterarguments. While the dispute never ends, this need not be schismatic. The only thing on which everyone will agree is that truth is best approached gradually, by means of rigorous argumentation; this is all part of God's plan.

Our Bible Is All about Us

The oral Torah combines the best of continuous and complete revelation. On the one hand, it ensures that revelation can be supplemented on demand, so as to keep it up-to-date. On the other hand, all past, present, and future readings are included in one and the same covenant made at Sinai. So, you don't invent new interpretations; you discover them. Situational as they all are, each and every interpretation is nonetheless part of an eternal, unchanging truth. The rabbis were quite firm about this: the law "is not in heaven" (Deut 30:12); Moses received from God everything anyone will ever need. There will be no second Testament.

The world changes, yet the word of God should be the same yesterday and today and forever. This is a key challenge to all scriptural religions. Religions do in fact transform over time. Christianity, for example, departed from Judaism and has ever since gone on to divide into new movements, some of which are recognizably Christian and others not. Yet however novel a doctrine or practice, those who introduced it typically prefer to regard it as scriptural. Often this means that the nature of the Scriptures is considered anew: what used to be a divine blueprint for a proper way of life becomes a prophecy that is just about to be fulfilled, for example. For the early Christians, the Jewish sacred Scriptures were first and foremost predictions about the Messiah—predictions they believed had come true with Jesus. In Luke's gospel, Jesus opens his public ministry with a piece of biblical commentary that leaves little open to interpretation. With reference to a passage in the book of Isaiah, he says:

> Today this scripture has been fulfilled in your hearing. (Luke 4:21)

Toward the end of the same Gospel, we hear him repeat:

> These are my words that I spoke to you while I was still with you—that everything written about me in the law of Moses, the prophets, and the psalms must be fulfilled. (Luke 24:44)

Between these two lines there is many an occasion that what was foretold about Jesus by the prophets comes true. Ostensibly a biography of Jesus, the gospel is a Christian commentary on the Jewish Scriptures. It uncovers their true, hidden meaning.

Yet the early Christians were not the only ones to reassess the Scriptures in light of their recent experience. In Qumran, by the Dead Sea, an extensive library of texts belonging to another Jewish eschatological group was discovered in 1947. Established in the second century BCE, this group was apparently part of a movement known as the Essenes. They, too, were convinced that the Bible was full of prophecies about them, about their spiritual leader called "the teacher of righteousness," and about their vile antagonists, the "children of darkness." Like the Christians, they picked up suitable passages from the law, the prophets, and the psalms, took them out of context, and reinterpreted them as prophecies they believed were currently coming true in their midst.

Strong as the Essenes were in their faith, their expectations went unrewarded. The Romans destroyed the Qumran community in the year 68.

Since then, different Jewish and Christian (and later, Muslim) groups have developed a variety of methods to decrypt secret knowledge assumedly hidden in the Bible (or the Quran). Among the most imaginative of these are gematria and the so-called Bible codes or "equidistant letter sequences."

Gematria is a system of assigning a numerical value to every Hebrew (or Greek, Arabic, Latin, or some other) alphabet, so as to interpret texts by means of the ensuing mathematical qualities. The rabbis were already familiar with this procedure. For example, we learn from Genesis that when Abram's nephew Lot was kidnapped, Abram went in pursuit of the captors with 318 trained men (Gen 14:14). According to a rabbinic interpretation, however, the actual count of men was only one. In case you should wonder who that was: the numerical value of Eliezer, Abram's valued servant, is exactly 318.

There is a well-known gematrical application for the Christian New Testament as well. The book of Revelation invites the reader to calculate the number of a satanic end-time beast, "for it is the number of a person" (Rev 13:18). The number in concern is 666. In the most common interpretation, this is a hidden reference to Emperor Nero, a persecutor of Christians.

Another means of extracting meaningful messages from the Bible, equidistant letter sequences (ELS) are, as the term implies, words and sentences formed by picking up letters in the text at regular intervals. To pick up a famous example, take every fifteenth letter of Genesis starting from the first letter *taw*, and the outcome will read the Hebrew word "Torah." Repeat this with Exodus, Numbers, or Deuteronomy, and the result will be the same. Weird or what?

In the computer age, gematria and ELS have reached entirely new dimensions. Thanks to appropriate software, the Bible is allegedly known to have predicted quite an array of things—ranging from nuclear weapons to the demise of the Soviet Union. With products on offer, anyone can now search the Scriptures for prophecies about themselves and their loved ones. Biblical interpretation has become as personal as it can get.

The Spirit and the Letter

It is with difficult texts in particular that learned, or creative, interpretations come in handy, as they can make dense passages comprehensible and point out new applications for ancient teachings. Yet sometimes texts can be difficult even if their message was crystal clear. We may find the ideas they propagate primitive, or outright immoral: how can anyone propose anything like that? In some biblical books, such passages abound—to the extent that critics of religion have found the biblical God guilty of crimes against humanity. Biblical instructions for a holy war, for example, are nothing short of a blueprint for complete ethnic cleansing:

> But as for the towns of these peoples that the Lord your God is giving you as an inheritance, you must not let anything that breathes remain alive. (Deut 20:16)

Problems posed by such texts of terror are not new. When Christianity first departed from Judaism, the Jewish sacred Scriptures (now renamed the Christian Old Testament) were soon to cause them trouble. Many Christians regarded those writings as alien and outdated, even more so as the emerging would-be New Testament literature began to establish itself. Messianic prophecies, monotheism, or demands for social justice were not a problem at all. Yet there were other things in the Old Testament that seemed odd or were in apparent contradiction to authentic Christian teaching. Paul, remember, had long since distanced himself from the Jewish ritual commandments:

> But now we are discharged from the law, dead to that which held us captive, so that we are slaves not under the old written code but in the new life of the Spirit. (Rom 7:6)

The Old Testament God was strange, too. What had this cruel and capricious tyrant to do with Jesus' heavenly father? Not much, many would say. Among them was Marcion, a second-century wealthy shipowner from Sinope in Pontus, Asia Minor. He, for one, was willing to let the Jewish Scriptures go. In their stead, he proposed a new canon of his own: a version of Luke's gospel (revised by Marcion himself) and a selection of Paul's letters. When the bishops in Rome were not in his favor, he set up his own church—which did not turn out badly at all but thrived more than a century. Who knows what Christianity would look like today, if it had not been for the Marcionite commitment to complete celibacy.

Yet Marcion had made what many considered a valid point. If the Old Testament was to remain in the Christian canon, it had to be read in a Christian way. This was, eventually, greatly helped by *allegorical interpretation*, pioneered by Origen (ca. 185–ca. 254). Origen modeled his approach on the Jewish philosopher Philo of Alexandria (born 10–15 BCE and died some sixty years later), who had earlier put allegory into extensive use. Philo's project was to prove that the Jewish religion was fully compatible with Greek philosophy. The Scriptures were not about historical truths but timeless ones:

> Now probably there was an actual man called Samuel; but we conceive of the Samuel of the scripture, not as a living compound of soul and body, but as a mind which rejoices in the service and worship of God and that only.[1]

Following Philo, Origen stated that while there was no reason to doubt the historical veracity of the Old Testament Scriptures, their literal meaning

---

1. Philo, *On Drunkenness*, 144.

was nonetheless secondary. What mattered was their figurative, spiritual sense as typologies and allegories of Jesus, the Christian church, the holy sacraments, the human soul, and its spiritual journey to the kingdom of heaven.

The crossing of the Red Sea in Exodus 14, for example, was a metaphor of baptism: just as the Israelites miraculously escaped the Pharaoh's troops, so are human souls pursued by demons yet saved by virtue of sheltering water. Whereas the literal meaning of the narrative was historical and transient, its spiritual sense remained as topical as ever, for all people, in all ages.

In medieval times, the distinction of the letter and the spirit became the bedrock of biblical interpretation. It went, ingeniously, hand in hand with the doctrine of the incarnation: in the beginning was the word, the eternal spiritual meaning of the Scriptures; later, that word became flesh in the actual words of the biblical text. Yet the material form and the spiritual content were not to be confused. Their relation was like that between body and soul. As the immortal soul was of far higher quality than the terrestrial body, so greatly did the spiritual meaning of the Bible transcend its plain literal sense.

The same principle applied not only to the Old Testament, but to the New as well. Take, for example, the memorable Good Samaritan. Luke tells a well-known story about a scribe who put Jesus to a test:

> "Teacher," he said, "what must I do to inherit eternal life?" He said to him: "What is written in the law? What do you read there?" He answered, "You shall love the Lord your God with all your heart, and with all your soul, and with all your strength, and with all your mind; and your neighbor as yourself." And he said to him, "You have given the right answer; do this, and you will live."
>
> But wanting to justify himself, he asked Jesus, "And who is my neighbor?" (Luke 10:25–29)

In response to this question, Jesus answered with the story of the Good Samaritan:

> "A man was going down from Jerusalem to Jericho, and fell into the hands of robbers, who stripped him, beat him, and went away, leaving him half dead. Now by chance a priest was going down that road; and when he saw him, he passed by on the other side. So likewise a Levite, when he came to the place and saw him, passed by on the other side. But a Samaritan while traveling came near

him; and when he saw him, he was moved with pity. He went to him and bandaged his wounds, having poured oil and wine on them. Then he put him on his own animal, brought him to an inn, and took care of him. The next day he took out two denarii, gave them to the innkeeper, and said, 'Take care of him; and when I come back, I will repay you whatever more you spend.' Which of these three, do you think, was a neighbor to the man who fell in the hands of the robbers?" He said, "The one who showed him mercy." Jesus said to him, "Go and do likewise." (Luke 10:30–37)

At face value, this is an exemplary story about the core essence of the Jewish law. The external holiness of the priest and the Levite is no good. What is decisive is how you respond to the suffering of other people. Therefore, even an infidel (as the Jews thought of the Samaritans) can exemplify God's will by showing mercy.

In a deeper sense, however, the story is about something else entirely. It is the details that provide the reader with keys to its true, spiritual content. As the Holy Spirit does not play dice, even the minutest feature must have a special meaning. The traveler's ill fate in the hands of the robbers is an image of humanity harassed by Satan and his lot. The man is Adam, exiled from paradise (Jerusalem) and headed towards the world (Jericho). The Samaritan is Christ, the inn is his church, and the promise to return refers to his second coming, the parousia. Adam is stripped—from immortality, due to his falling into sin. While he is absolved through the sacraments (oil and wine), he remains in need of pastoral care until the Lord returns.

What Jesus Really Said

Allegorical interpretation of sacred texts is by no means an exclusively Jewish or Christian phenomenon. It is, rather, a standard developmental phase when people of a religious tradition first come to consider their Scriptures primitive. To solve this problem, they regard certain features—that is, those that contradict their current morals and world view—as metaphoric. A genuinely historical understanding of religion as an evolving process will only come later.

The essential difference between ancient or medieval and modern biblical interpretation is in the sense of history. While the rabbis and Fathers were quite aware that the texts were in need of novel interpretations, they nevertheless regarded their meaning as positively ahistorical. Whatever readings you were to discover, they were all first given to Moses at Sinai, or the Holy Spirit had planted them in the text at the beginning of time. This was why the Scriptures had the power to impress people regardless of time and culture.

Modern times were different. The Renaissance, Reformation, and Enlightenment rejected allegorical interpretation and emphasized the literal, historical meaning of the Scriptures. Readings should match the actual, empirical features of the text and not the other way round. This paved the way for the modern, historical-critical method of biblical interpretation.

Modern research has its own recipe for making sense of awkward texts. Today's scholars look at the original context. In what kind of social and cultural conditions did the text first emerge? What sorts of topical issues were people struggling with? What now seems incomprehensible, primitive, or inappropriate, may not always have been so. In their original historical setting, even the weirdest of writings may appear in a different light. This can only happen, however, if we first realize that the texts were not written for a twentieth (or sixteenth, or eleventh) century audience. Between them and us yawns a chasm that needs to be crossed by means of informed, critical reading.

The first step is that we recognize the irreversible otherness of the text. This requires courage, as it means that we cannot know for sure if the text will have any relevance today. Whatever its message was for its first readers, that (or any other) reading may not have a bearing on our present-day situation at all.

Yet historical knowledge can be of great help in making the Scriptures more accessible. A fine example of this was provided by the late, sagacious theologian and biblical scholar Walter Wink. He was troubled over some implications of Jesus' Sermon of the Mount, until he realized who Jesus' audience was and how they would have understood his words. The passage that worried Wink the most was Jesus' teaching concerning retaliation:

> You have heard that it was said, "An eye for an eye and a tooth for a tooth." But I say to you, Do not resist an evildoer. But if anyone strikes you on the right cheek, turn the other also; and if anyone wants to sue you and take your coat, give your cloak as well; and if anyone forces you to go one mile, go also the second mile. Give to everyone who begs from you, and do not refuse anyone who wants to borrow from you. (Matt 5:38–42; cf. Luke 6:29–30)

Was Jesus proposing that we give in to injustice and oppression? This is indeed how his message is often understood. Many people have taken Jesus' words as an extreme example of self-denial. The righteous will enter through the narrow gate and take the hard road that leads to martyrdom.

But will that not serve the interests of dictators and tyrants? How will the world ever change if no one stands up against oppressors? Besides, what right has anyone to call the oppressed to renounce their human dignity? Fortunately, said Wink, Jesus taught nothing of that sort. Once we realize who his audience was, we will see that his point was not passive submission but nonviolent resistance.

Like the rabbis and Fathers, Wink, too, looked at the seemingly redundant details of the text. Why, for example, did Jesus mention *the right cheek* in particular?

To strike someone on the right cheek requires that you either use your left hand or the back of you right one. In biblical times, the left hand was out of question, because it was only used for impure purposes. No honorable person would risk the shame of touching someone with the left hand. So it must be the back of the right hand, then. Now, that kind of strike carried a special meaning. It was used in order to put a person in his or her place. That was how a master would strike a slave; a man his wife; and how parents struck their children. Jesus was talking to people who were struck on the right cheek due to their class, gender, age, or nationality. For them, turning the other cheek was a meaningful gesture—a bold demand to be treated as equal.

What about the call to give, not only your coat but your cloak as well? Who would sue someone to claim their clothes? And which piece of clothing is it, as herein Matthew and Luke will not agree? Matthew writes, "and if anyone wants to sue you and take your coat, give your cloak as well" (Matt 5:40), whereas Luke has it: "and from anyone who takes away your coat do not withhold even your shirt" (Luke 6:29).

According to Wink, Luke has it right. It is the outerwear that is being claimed. The Hebrew Bible contains several examples of taking someone's cloak in pawn:

> If you lend money to my people, to the poor among you, you shall not deal with them as a creditor; you shall not exact interest from them. If you take your neighbor's cloak in pawn, you shall restore it before the sun goes down; for it may be your neighbor's only clothing to use as cover; in what else shall that person sleep? And

if your neighbor cries out to me, I will listen, for I am compassionate. (Ex 22:25–27; cf. Deut 24:10–13, 17; Amos 2:6–8)

Again, Jesus' words imply who his addressees were: only the poorest of the poor have nothing but their cloak to pawn.

So, why did Jesus advise to give the shirt as well—that is, to go naked in front of the court of law? Again, we are dealing with issues of honor and shame. Public nudity was a shameful sight. The gesture Jesus proposed would have shown the true colors of oppression. There is no honor in greed. To take advantage of the poor is a crime against human dignity. Shame on anyone who is found guilty of that!

What about going the extra mile, then? At this point, Jesus was actually talking about a special case, that is, the forced labor imperial soldiers were authorized to require of those under Roman occupation. A case like this is, in fact, mentioned elsewhere in the New Testament: "They compelled a passer-by, who was coming in from the country, to carry [Jesus'] cross; it was Simon of Cyrene, the father of Alexander and Rufus" (Mark 15:21; cf. Matt 27:32). This was standard practice known in Judea and Galilee since Persian times. Anyone might be called to duty. Usually you would be forced to provide a beast of burden or help carry a soldier's gear.

This practice—known by the Persian word *angareia*—was essential when large and heavily armed units were moved to remote parts of the empire. At the same time, it was a heavy burden for their population and could easily feed anti-Roman sentiment. It was therefore strictly limited: one mile, not two. In other words, oppression should be measured and proportionate. Transgressions of this rule were punished swiftly and severely.

Jesus' advice to volunteer the second mile jams the machine. The soldier has lost control. If he is suspected of going off limits, he will receive punishment. If the civilian dies, he may even be executed. On the other hand, if he tried to take his gear back by force, the civilian might accuse him of assault—and who would ever believe him if he said he only tried to force the poor man *not* to help? So, should he run up to him and talk sense to him? Whatever the way, he will only end up looking ridiculous.

Jesus' witty words are crisis therapy for the abused. His message comes through loud and clear. You are entitled to human dignity. Shame is not on you. Stand up for your rights.

The Silent Word

Wink's reading is a success: it makes good sense of a difficult text. It paints a portrait of Jesus that liberal moderns, too, can readily accept: a social revolutionary, human rights defender, pioneer of nonviolent resistance. This kind of Jesus might even attract followers from the radical left.

Unlike allegorical interpretation, however, historical readings cannot be trusted to absolve any text that seems in need of repair. Sometimes primitive, cruel, or sexist texts are just primitive, cruel, and sexist. The Bible is a creature of its age, and a mirror image of human nature, for better and for worse.

Thanks to critical research, we are now better aware than ever of the human limitations of our sacred literature. Libraries full of manuscripts testify that we have not one but many "original" versions of the texts, and even the most reliable ones will not fully agree. Furthermore, most biblical books have a long editorial history. One hand after another has worked on them, making corrections, omissions, and additions, so that the finished product consists of a number of layers dating back to different authors and traditions from different historical periods.

Also, as we saw before, we have come to realize how profoundly different the biblical culture and world view were from our own. Severely at odds as they can be with what we now know about human nature and behavior, it would be unethical to base our moral judgment blindly on them.

In other words, the biblical text hardly qualifies as God's eternal word (a role most Christians would assign to Christ only, anyway). An idealized image of the Bible as historically or morally inerrant only implies that we are lamentably unfamiliar with its content—or that we are simply in denial.

On the other hand, the idea of the Bible's irredeemably human nature (along with its divine inspiration) has always been a sturdy part of the Christian tradition. Biblical inerrancy in a literal sense remains a minority position. No Christian would worship the Bible like some worship the Sacred Host. And while pious Jews say the Torah was made in heaven, and pious Muslims claim the same of the Holy Quran, Christians have always considered their Bible merely a divinely inspired work of human hands.

A number of early church fathers actually made a point of how unrefined their sacred literature was. For Tatian, Justin Martyr, Tertullian, and Origen, the power of the Bible was perfected in its weakness. The biblical authors hardly excelled in rhetorical skill, yet they were able to convince countless readers. If that wasn't a sign of divine authority, what is? Surely unfiltered truth needs no oratorical trickery in its support.

The Fathers were only building on Paul's earlier, antirhetorical polemics. This is the apostle speaking to the church in Corinth:

> When I came to you, brothers and sisters, I did not come proclaiming the mystery of God to you in lofty words of wisdom.... My speech and my proclamation were not with plausible words of wisdom, but with a demonstration of the Spirit and power, so that your faith might rest not on human wisdom but on the power of God. (1 Cor 2:1, 4–5)

As much of a rhetorical understatement as that may be, many would later appeal to it. Bible translations became typical occasions for debate: should they be the crown jewels of each national canon of literature, or rather treasures in clay jars, free of literary ambition, exclusively concerned with the spiritual contents of God's eternal word?

How exactly do human words and God's revealed truth meet in the biblical text? The ancient rabbis already found this a fascinating question. True to their habits, they turned to the Bible for answers (and now I must again acknowledge my debt to Visotzky's treasury of Talmudic anecdotes). The rabbis noticed that, at Sinai, it was God himself who spoke the first two commandments:

> I am the Lord your God, who brought you out of the land of Egypt, out of the house of slavery; you shall have no other gods before me.
> You shall not make for yourself an idol, whether in the form of anything that is in heaven above, or that is on the earth beneath, or that is in the water under the earth. You shall not bow down to them or worship them; for I the Lord your God am a jealous God, punishing children for the iniquity of parents, to the third and the fourth generation of those who reject me, but showing steadfast love to the thousandth generation of those who love me and keep my commandments. (Exod 20:2–6)

Then, abruptly, God's speech was cut short. Another voice stepped in to introduce the remaining eight commandments, speaking of God in the third person: "You shall not make wrongful use of the name of the Lord your God, for the Lord will not acquit anyone who misuses his name" (Exod 20:7), and so on. From this the rabbis inferred that only the first two commandments were the word of God. That was as much as the people could take. Terrified, they turned to Moses and said to him: "You speak to us, and we will listen; but do not let God speak to us, or we will die" (Exod 20:19). So it was Moses who spoke the rest.

A nineteenth-century Jewish mystic, Menahem Mendel, took this interpretation further with impeccable insight and a disarming sense of humor. He suggested that God never made it further than the first letter of the first commandment. This already was too much for the people, and Moses had to intercede. Now in the Hebrew text, that letter happens to be an aleph, and an aleph will only make a sound when accompanied by a vowel. In other words, God's own, genuine voice did indeed open the divine revelation we now have in the Bible—yet it comprised only a single letter, and a silent one at that.

7

Childish Ways

The Cloud of Unknowing

As a literary character, the biblical God grows and matures. From the garden of Eden to Mount Sinai, from Christ's birth in Bethlehem to his ascent from the Mount of Olives, it becomes all the more clear that God's proper place is not on earth but in heaven—which indeed is where he takes his residence in the end. We also learn that whatever we humans may think or say about God can, at best, only approximate God's true nature. While God is eternal and ageless, even our most sacred literature is transient and mutable, conditioned by the contingencies of language, history, culture, and the human mind.

To what, then, shall we compare the biblical character of God? He is like a cocoon from which the real God eventually emerges, ready to take his wings, leaving behind an empty shelf with an imprint of his image: God was here.

What the Bible does is picture an image of an unimaginable God. Words give way to the unspeakable. By way of literature, the Bible replicates the standard mystical experience: en route to God, all mental images gradually vanish into thin air. Like the mystic, the reader will understand that God's reality is infinitely beyond human imagination. In the language of the Christian mystical tradition, "the dark night of the soul" comes on and covers the human consciousness in "a cloud of unknowing." A title of a classic work in medieval English mysticism, the last mentioned metaphor is a biblical one. When Moses went up to God at Sinai, God came to him "in a dense cloud" (Exod 19:9).

Increasingly real, God grows vague in outline. Hidden in a cloud, he remains outside human comprehension, lest Creator be mistaken for creation:

> Since you saw no form when the Lord spoke to you at Horeb out of the fire, take care and watch yourselves closely, so that you do not act corruptly by making an idol for yourselves, in the form of any figure—the likeness of male or female, the likeness of any animal that is on the earth, the likeness of any winged bird that flies in the air, the likeness of anything that creeps on the ground, the likeness of any fish that is in the water under the earth. And when you look up to the heavens and see the sun, the moon, and the stars, all the host of heaven, do not be led astray and bow down to them and serve them, things that the Lord your God has allotted to all the peoples everywhere under heaven. (Deut 4:15–19)

In a similar vein, the literary God is veiled in the likeness of human nature. What we learn of him and how depends on his historical, cultural, narrative, and psychological habitat. No divine image or revelation as untouched by human hand was ever given to anyone, not even in the holy Bible. It is imperative that we understand this, as it will effectively protect us against religion become evil. Since no one has the privilege of knowing God completely, all religious ideas and practices are to be assessed freely on the basis of their practical implications and internal coherence:

> but test everything; hold fast to what is good; abstain from every form of evil. (1 Thess 5:21–22)

> Beware of false prophets, who come to you in sheep's clothing but inwardly are ravenous wolves. You will know them by their fruits. Are grapes gathered from thorns, or figs from thistles? In the same way, every good tree bears good fruit, but the bad tree bears bad fruit. (Matt 7:15–17)

Even the Bible shows God only "in a mirror, dimly," not face-to-face (1 Cor 13:12). Yet it succeeds in taking God's story to the point where God's emerging reality calls for silence. As the formless God approached people in the visible form of fire at Horeb, so does God's character in the Bible traffic transcendence to us humans, smuggle it into our limited, immanent world—albeit in a hidden form, and only to be given up again as soon as we discover God's true colors.

The true God is ineffable. Therefore, his figure will eventually dissolve into a limitless presence. This is the key moment of all mystical experience, the goal of the mystic's ardent spiritual labor: to give up limited, inadequate images of God; to cease to be misled by them; to experience God as pure being. As the figure of God finally disappears from sight, the divine presence takes over everything. In the words of the psalmist:

> If I ascend to heaven, you are there;
> if I make my bed in Sheol, you are there.
> If I take the wings of the morning
> and settle at the farthest limits of the sea,
> even there your hand shall lead me,
> and your right hand shall hold me fast.
> If I say, "Surely the darkness shall cover me,
> and the light around me become night,"
> even the darkness is not dark to you;
> the night is as bright as the day,
> for darkness is as light to you.
> (Ps 139:8–12)

Too Old for Imaginary Friends?

So, was the biblical narrative all an illusion? Is the biblical character of God simply one of those childish things we should put away when we grow up? In the sense that God must be far greater than any particular human vision of God, the answer must be a resounding yes. Yet this need not be the whole story. In life, childish ways, too, have a purpose—so perhaps Jesus had a point when he said that whoever does not receive the kingdom of God as a little child will never enter it (Mark 10:15)? Even faith in the ineffable comes from what is heard (Rom 10:17). Partial and incomplete as it is, human imagination remains a singular gateway to life beyond the apparent.

Some say the best things in life are illusions that we are not supposed to put away. Self-esteem, love, and a sense of belonging are all based on something other than cold facts, yet it is essential that we take them for real. In a broader sense, the same is true of art, culture, and indeed, religion. They all involve experienced reality furnished with personal meaning in a way that, technically, is an illusion. Yet it hardly makes sense to call them deceptions or lies. What, then, is at play?

When the American Humanist Association put up the campaign, "Too Old for Imaginary Friends," they perhaps unwittingly put their finger on a key point. Targeted at children and teenagers, the campaign ads featured young teens looking dismissively at a finger pointing at them from the clouds. Below, a text read "I'm getting a bit old for imaginary friends." Now, imaginary friends belong to a realm of psychic life the British psychoanalyst D.W. Winnicott called *the transitional phenomena*. Special extensions of the self, they stand halfway between inner experience and outer reality. Winnicott initially introduced this concept with reference to a particular developmental sequence: a typical example of a transitional object is a safety blanket or a soft toy that comes to be of special importance to an infant. Later, however, Winnicott expanded the idea into a broader vision of mental health and creativity. Giving birth to art and culture, transitional experience makes us able to connect our inner experience of the self with the world of other self-conscious beings.

A key thing about the transitional phenomena is that their reality, outside fantasy, is not to be challenged. To ask if the teddy bear is really what the child conceives it to be is to miss the point. The child is not lying or hallucinating. Instead, he or she is takings steps from the early, illusory experience of the world as created by the child's own wishes to the actual world that exists on its own right, independently of the child. As the transition progresses and the child builds capacity to trust the external world, the transitional object is left behind. The child has grown too old for imaginary friends like the teddy bear, the invisible playmate, or the old man in the clouds.

Yet this is not the end of story for transitional phenomena. Later in life, art, culture, and religion perform a similar function. Their point, too, is not to make positive, verifiable statements of the external reality in the ordinary sense of the word. Rather, they constitute a protected realm for creative vision and play that is vital for our being in touch with ourselves and for our relatedness with others. The illusion of art and religion is not a way to escape or avoid reality but a means to access it personally.

Winnicott and other British object relations theorists are part of a psychoanalytic tradition that redefined the concept of illusion. Earlier, Melanie Klein had called into question Freud's clear-cut distinction between childish fantasies and a mature sense of reality. And there are other instrumental cases as well. In the United States, Heinz Kohut's self-psychology is another good example.

For Freud, idealization and narcissism were childish features to be outgrown: everyone must learn that the world does not turn around us. For Kohut, however, there was a positive side to them that remained relevant throughout one's entire life. In order to be well, people need to be able to feel that they, their loved ones, and their communities are special. This is not something directed by the reality principle: objectively speaking, no part of reality is any more special, blessed, or meaningful than any other. Yet, such a feeling of worth is hardly delusional, either. It is rather something no one can live without: we need what Kohut called self-objects, special people, places, and things that help us sustain a sense of coherence and vitality. Religion provides for such experiences of positive idealization, as it proposes there is such a thing as the supreme good; that human beings are valuable and called to salvation; that all God's children are sisters and brothers to each other, and so on.

A Kind of Fiction?

So, not all childish things must be put away as we mature. Illusion and fantasy are not undesirable by definition.

Yet it is still illusion and fantasy we are talking about. How does that go together with real, lived religions, and real, living people of faith? Would they go so far as to call their sacred Scriptures, rituals, or relationship with the divine illusions? Isn't such an idea of a "mature religion" itself an idealization with no historical or empirical basis, rather like the "natural religion" of the deists, or, as Rachel Blass has wryly pointed out, like those Westernized, meditation-oriented interpretations of Buddhism which so many analytics with a Winnicottian twist nowadays hold dear. Against them Blass quotes the theologian Hans Küng:

> The man who believes . . . is primarily interested . . . in the reality itself. . . . He wants to know whether and to what extent his faith is based on illusion or on historical reality. Any faith based on illusion is not really faith but superstition.[1]

Freud himself accounted for a discussion like this, noting that a philosopher might view religion as a kind of fiction accepted as true for its practical

---

1. Blass, "Beyond Illusion," 33.

significance. However, he said, no serious believer would accept this. Küng just seemed to prove his point. Besides, Küng's words only echo a deeper source, as in 2 Peter:

> For we did not follow cleverly devised myths when we made known to you the power as coming of our Lord Jesus Christ, but we had been eyewitnesses of his majesty. (1:16)

So, it is a take it or leave it, then? Yes—first, in the sense that God, in order to be God, certainly must be real, more real than this reality can take, too real for the Bible itself to contain, save one silent letter aleph or what can be shown in a mirror, dimly. Every serious witness of God's majesty knows this, from the wisest among sages to the most humble commoner knelt before a plastic patron saint. God is something completely different, yet God makes the divine fit in the ordinary.

And so, second, yes, we must keep to the childish ways of addressing God in our deficient human language, because there is no other way. As Paul in his lovable condescending style reminds the church in Corinth, speaking in heavenly yet incomprehensible tongues is not much use for anyone. Glossolalia is no form of witness, unless someone translates it into something we humans can understand. And then of course, Paul does one of his finest moves, concluding that love is the language humans understand the best. (See 1 Cor 12 and 13.)

There is no other way than the imaginary, illusory, dim language of human faith, hope, and love. Moreover, that language does not fully translate into any other human language—such as the language of philosophy, ethics, psychology, or fiction. If the language of the sacred becomes lost, all that goes with it will be lost permanently, too. The Australian philosopher Raimond Gaita puts it well: "When certain ways of speaking go dead on us, we cannot necessarily extract our old thoughts from those ways of speaking, express them in an idiom more congenial to the present."[2]

This is the key question behind Nietzsche's famous dictum about the death of God. If our advanced understanding of the world should wean us from religion—if God leaves us for good, and we respond by ceasing to take our languages of illusion seriously—what will be different? What value does spirituality add to the secular, disenchanted, fully grown-up talk of good life as represented by the modern discourses of self-actualization, social responsibility, psychic well-being, and mental health?

---

2. Gaita, *A Common Humanity*, 235.

Some three decades ago, Paul Pruyser, an American clinical psychologist and keen analyst of religious imagination (with Winnicottian leanings) addressed this question in a small book, *The Minister as Diagnostician: Personal Problems in Pastoral Perspective*. For Pruyser, the question was a practical one. He had for long time worked in close association with pastors in clinical practice and training. Time and again, he had noticed how eager modern clergymen were to learn from psychologists and psychiatrists. They wanted to know how to give people adequate psychological support for their problems. Yet the kind of help those people hoped to get from them was quite different from what they'd expect from any other helping profession. They had spiritual needs no medical or psychotherapeutic treatment could meet. Those needs would be assessed by means of such questions as: what do you hold as sacred?; do you feel your life has a purpose?; what does faith mean to you?; can you think of your life as a gift?; what will you do when you have wronged others?; do you feel embedded in a larger communion of people, or perhaps of all living beings?; is what you do for living in harmony in line with what you think is right and worth doing? These kinds of questions could hardly be answered by medicine or psychology alone. This is because they are not merely questions of the mind and the body. Rather, they are questions of that ancient illusion known as the human soul.

Like a Weaned Child

How to address the needs of the soul—a strange mix of love, truth, beauty, justice, and compassion? By way of decrees, statutes, and ordinances? Yes, principles are certainly good—but beware of taking them too rigidly, lest they lead you think the world is black and white and make you merciless. Perhaps it would be wise to supply soul-seekers with proverbs and parables, to remind us that we should always learn from experience and be prepared to think things anew. Better add some dramatic stories as well—they will help us see how different things may look depending on your point of view. And some psalms of joy, awe, and lament also, for life is not all intellect but very much emotion; besides, how will we ever find a single answer, if our most intimate questions, our moments of doubt and inspiration, are not heard and acknowledged? In fact, for that very reason, even a drop of madness might have its place.

A genuinely holy book, the Bible is composed of all things shining, for the nourishment of the human soul. Yet at the same time, it is also properly dirty with all things human, for better and for worse. It is demandingly mature and blessedly childish. Its God rightly introduces himself as "I am who I am"—no compromises. At his hand we receive the good and the bad. He rubs our nose to the unyielding reality, yet sustains our faith in the wildest of ideals. He loads us with the burden of life and then gives us rest in its mystery. While none of us has ever gained sight of him, we still gather together to meet him and give him thanks. Separated, reared, and sent away to the world on our own, we still carry with us the memory of the time we slept, content, in his arms:

> But I have calmed and quieted my soul,
> like a weaned child with its mother;
> my soul is like the weaned child that is with me. (Ps 131:2)

Bibliography

Alter, Robert. *The Art of Biblical Narrative*. New York: Basic, 1981.
Auerbach, Erich. *Mimesis: The Representation of Reality in Western Literature*. Translated by Willard R. Trask. Princeton, NJ: Princeton University Press, 1968.
Bechtel, Lyn M. "Genesis 2.4b-3.24: A Myth about Human Maturation." *Journal for the Study of the Old Testament* 67 (1995) 3-26.
———. "Developmental Psychology in Biblical Studies." In *Psychology and the Bible: A New Way to Read the Scriptures, Vol. 1: From Freud to Kohut*, edited by J. Harold Ellens and Wayne G. Rollins, 119-38. Westport, CT: Praeger, 2004.
———. "Rethinking the Interpretation of Genesis 2.4b-3.24." In *The Feminist Companion to Genesis*, edited by Athalya Brenner, 77-117. Sheffield: JSOT Press, 1993.
Berger, Peter L., ed. *The Desecularization of the World: Resurgent Religion and World Politics*. Washington, DC: Ethics and Public Policy Center, 1999.
Black, David M., ed. *Psychoanalysis and Religion in the 21st Century: Competitors or Collaborators?* The New Library of Psychoanalysis. London: Routledge, 2006.
Blass, Rachel B. "Beyond Illusion: Psychoanalysis and the Question of Religious Truth." In *Psychoanalysis and Religion in the 21st Century: Competitors or Collaborators?*, edited by David M. Black, 23-43. London: Routledge, 2006.
Borg, Marcus J. *Jesus in Contemporary Scholarship*. Valley Forge, PA: Trinity Press International, 1994.
Brueggeman, Walter. "The Formfulness of Grief." *Interpretation* 31 (1977) 263-75.
Capps, Donald. "Beyond Schweitzer and the Psychiatrists: Jesus as Fictive Personality." In *Psychology and the Bible: A New Way to Read the Scriptures, Vol. 4: From Christ to Jesus*, edited by J. Harold Ellens and Wayne G. Rollins, 89-124. Westport, CT: Praeger, 2004.
———. *Biblical Approaches to Pastoral Counseling*. Philadelphia: Westminster, 1981.
Capps, Donald, ed. *Freud and Freudians on Religion: A Reader*. New Haven, CT: Yale University Press, 2001.
Caruth, Cathy. *Unclaimed Experience: Trauma, Narrative, and History*. Baltimore: Johns Hopkins University Press, 1996.
The Cloud of Unknowing and Other Works. Translated into modern English by Clifton Wolters. Harmondsworth: Penguin, 1980.
Cohn, Dorrit. *The Distinction of Fiction*. Baltimore: Johns Hopkins University Press, 1999.

BIBLIOGRAPHY

Conzelmann, Hans. *The Theology of St. Luke.* Translated by Geoffrey Buswell. London: SCM, 1982.

Crossan, John Dominic. *The Historical Jesus: The Life of a Mediterranean Jewish Peasant.* New York: HarperCollins, 1992.

———. *Jesus: A Revolutionary Biography.* New York: HarperCollins, 1994.

Darr, John A. *On Character Building: The Reader and the Rhetoric of Characterization in Luke-Acts.* Louisville: Westminster John Knox, 1992.

DeConick, April D. *Holy Misogyny: Why the Sex and Gender Conflicts in the Early Church Still Matter.* New York: Continuum, 2011.

Drosnin, Michael. *The Bible Code.* New York: Simon & Schuster, 1997.

Dunn, James D. G. *Unity and Diversity in the New Testament: An Inquiry into the Character of Earliest Christianity.* London: SCM, 1997.

Eagleton, Terry. *Reason, Faith, and Revolution: Reflections on the God Debate.* The Terry Lecture Series. New Haven, CT: Yale University Press, 2009.

Eco, Umberto. *Six Walks in the Fictional Woods.* Cambridge, MA: Harvard University Press, 1994.

Epictetus. *The Discourses as Reported by Arrian, the Manual, and Fragments.* Translated by William A. Oldfather. The Loeb Classical Library, book 131, no. 218. Cambridge, MA: Harvard University Press, 1959–61.

Erkkilä, Leena. *Kukkutimurusia: Satuja.* Porvoo: WSOY, 1968.

Felman, Shoshana, and Dori Laub. *Testimony: The Crisis of Witnessing in Literature, Psychoanalysis, and History.* New York: Routledge, 1992.

Freud, Sigmund. *Civilization and Its Discontents.* Translated by David McLintock. London: Penguin, 2002.

———. *The Future of an Illusion.* Newly translated and edited by James Strachey. New York: Norton, 1975.

Friedman, Richard Elliott. *The Hidden Face of God.* New York: HarperCollins, 1995.

Gaita, Raimond. *A Common Humanity: Thinking about Love and Truth and Justice.* London: Routledge, 2000.

Garber, David G., Jr. "Traumatizing Ezekiel, the Exilic Prophet." In *Psychology and the Bible: A New Way to Read the Scriptures, Vol. II: From Genesis to Apocalyptic Vision,* edited by J. Harold Ellens and Wayne G. Rollins, 215–35. Westport, CT: Praeger, 2004.

Gascoigne, Bamber. *The Christians.* With photographs by Christina Gascoigne. A Channel Four book. London: Cape, 1986.

Gennep, Arnold van. *The Rites of Passage.* Translated by Monika B. Vizedom and Gabrielle L. Caffee. Chicago: University of Chicago Press, 1960.

Geyer, Douglas. "Disavowing the Gospel While Believing It." Unpublished paper presented at the Society of Biblical Literature annual meeting, 2001.

Gospel of Thomas. In *The Nag Hammadi Library in English,* edited by James M. Robinson, 124–38. San Francisco: Harper & Row, 1988.

Grant, Patrick. *Imperfection.* Cultural Dialectics. Edmonton: AU Press, 2012.

Hood, Ralph W., Jr. "Psychoanalysis and Fundamentalism: A Lesson from Feminist Critiques of Freud." In *Religion, Society, and Psychoanalysis: Readings in Contemporary Theory,* edited by Janet Liebman Jacobs and Donald Capps, 42–67. Boulder, CO: Westview, 1997.

BIBLIOGRAPHY

Hopkins, Brooke. "Jesus and Object Use: A Winnicottian Account of the Resurrection Myth." In *Freud and Freudians on Religion: A Reader*, edited by Donald Capps, 230–40. New Haven, CT: Yale University Press, 2001.

Humphreys, Colin J. *The Miracles of Exodus: A Scientist's Discovery of the Extraordinary Natural Causes of Biblical Stories*. New York: Continuum.

Jacobs, Janet Liebman, and Donald Capps, eds. *Religion, Society, and Psychoanalysis: Readings in Contemporary Theory*. Boulder, CO: Westview, 1997.

James, Rick. "What is Distinctive About FBOs? How European FBOs define and operationalize their faith." Praxis Paper 22. Oxford: Intrac, 2009.

Jeremias, Joachim. *New Testament Theology: Part 1, The Proclamation of Jesus*. The New Testament Library. London: SCM, 1971.

Jones, James W. *Contemporary Psychoanalysis and Religion: Transference and Transcendence*. New Haven, CT: Yale University Press, 1991.

———. *Terror and Transformation: The Ambiguity of Religion in Psychoanalytic Perspective*. New York: Brunner-Routledge, 2002.

———. *Toward a Relational Psychoanalysis of Religion*. New Haven, CT: Yale University Press, 1996.

Juan de la Cruz. *The Collected Works of Saint John of the Cross*. Translated by Kieran Kavanaugh and Otilio Rodriguez. Washington, DC: ICS Publications, 1991.

The Judas Gospel @ National Geographic Magazine. http://www7.nationalgeographic.com/ngm/gospel/index.html

Kermode, Frank. *The Genesis of Secrecy: On the Interpretation of Narrative*. Cambridge, MA: Harvard University Press, 1979.

Kille, D. Andrew. "'The Bible Made Me Do It:' Text, Interpretation and Violence." In *The Destructive Power of Religion*, edited by J. Harold Ellens, 55–73. Westport, CT: Praeger, 2004.

———. *Psychological Biblical Criticism*. Guides to Biblical Scholarship: Old Testament Series. Minneapolis: Fortress, 2001.

Kimball, Charles. *When Religion Becomes Evil*. New York: HarperSanFrancisco, 2002.

Kohut, Heinz. *The Analysis of the Self: A Systematic Approach to the Psychoanalytic Treatment of Narcissistic Personality Disorders*. The Psychoanalytic Study of the Child Monograph Series 4. New York: International Universities Press, 1971.

———. *How Does Analysis Cure?* Chicago: University of Chicago Press, 1984.

Kübler-Ross, Elizabeth. *On Death and Dying*. New York: Macmillan, 1969.

Küng, Hans. *On Being a Christian*. Translated by E. Quinn. New York: Image, 1984.

Laqueur, Thomas. *Making Sex: Body and Gender from the Greeks to Freud*. Cambridge, MA: Harvard University Press, 1990.

Malina, Bruce J. *The New Testament World: Insights from Cultural Anthropology*. London: SCM, 1981.

Malina, Bruce J., and Richard L. Rohrbaugh. *Social Science Commentary on the Synoptic Gospels*. Minneapolis: Fortress, 1992.

Mamet, David. *A Whore's Profession: Notes and Essays*. London: Faber and Faber, 1994.

Marjanen, Antti. "How Egalitarian Was the Gnostic View of Women? Mary Magdalene Texts in the Nag Hammadi and Related Documents." In *Coptic Studies on the Threshold of a New Millennium: Proceedings of the Seventh International Congress of Coptic Studies, Leiden, August 27–September 2, 2000*, edited by M. Immerzeel, J. van der Vliet, M. Kersten, and C. van Zoest, 785–97. Orientalia Lovaniensia Analecta 133. Louvain: Peeters, 2004.

BIBLIOGRAPHY

———. *The Woman Jesus Loved: Mary Magdalene in the Nag Hammadi Library and Related Documents*. Nag Hammadi and Manichaean Studies 40. Leiden: Brill, 1996.

———. "Women Disciples in Thomas." In *Thomas at the Crossroads: Essays on the Gospel of Thomas*, edited by Risto Uro, 89–106. Edinburgh: T & T Clark, 1998.

Marshall, Katherine. "Religious literacy crucial to understand Pakistan flood response, mosque debate." *The Washington Post*, August 23, 2010. http://newsweek.washingtonpost.com/onfaith/georgetown/2010/08/religious_literacy_crucial_to_understand_pakistan_flood_response_mosque_debate.html#more.

Marx, Karl. *Critique of Hegel's Philosophy of Right*. Translated by A. Jolin and J. O'Malley. Cambridge Studies in the History and Theory of Politics. Cambridge: Cambridge University Press, 1970.

Meissner, William W. *Psychoanalysis and Religious Experience*. New Haven, CT: Yale University Press, 1984.

Merenlahti, Petri. "Distorted Reality or Transitional Space? Biblical Miracle Stories in Psychoanalytic Perspective." In *Miracles: God, Science, and Psychology in the Paranormal, Vol. 1: Religious and Spiritual Events*, edited by J. Harold Ellens, 15–35. Westport, CT: Praeger, 2008.

———. "Divine Desires: Fantasy and Renunciation in the Narrative of Mark's Gospel." In *Sacred Marriages: The Divine-Human Sexual Metaphor from Sumer to Early Christianity*, edited by Martti Nissinen and Risto Uro, 411–36. Winona Lake, IN: Eisenbrauns, 2008.

———. *Poetics for the Gospels? Rethinking Narrative Criticism*. London: T & T Clark, 2002.

———. "Reading as a Little Child: On the Model Reader of the Gospels." *Literature & Theology* 18 (2004) 139–52.

———. "So Who Really Needs Therapy? On Psychological Exegesis and Its Subject." *Svensk exegetisk årsbok* 72 (2007) 7–30.

Meyer, Marvin W., ed. *The Nag Hammadi Scriptures*. New York: HarperOne, 2007.

Micklethwait, John, and Adrian Wooldridge. *God Is Back: How the Global Rise of Faith Will Change the World*. New York: Penguin, 2009.

Miles, Jack. *Christ: A Crisis in the Life of God*. New York: Alfred A. Knopf, 2001.

———. *God: A Biography*. New York: Alfred A. Knopf, 1995.

Mitchell, Stephen A., and Margaret J. Black. *Freud and Beyond: A History of Modern Psychoanalytic Thought*. New York: Basic, 1995.

"The Mythology of Star Wars with George Lucas and Bill Moyers." VHS, color, 57 min. Distributed by Films for the Humanities and Sciences, Princeton, NJ. Produced by Pamela Mason Wagner, 1999.

Norton, David. *A History of the Bible as Literature*, 2 vols. Cambridge: Cambridge University Press, 1993.

Orsi, Robert A. *Between Heaven and Earth: The Religious Worlds People Make and the Scholars Who Study Them*. Princeton, NJ: Princeton University Press, 2005.

——— *The Madonna of 115th Street: Faith and Community in Italian Harlem, 1880–1950*. New Haven, CT: Yale University Press, 2010.

Otto, Rudolf. *The Idea of the Holy: An Inquiry into the Non-Rational Factor in the Idea of the Divine and Its Relation to the Rational*. Translated by J. W. Harvey. London: Oxford University Press, 1917.

Parsons, Terence. *Nonexistent Objects*. New Haven, CT: Yale University Press, 1980.

BIBLIOGRAPHY

Paulus, H. E. G. *Das Leben Jesu als Grundlage einer reinen Geschichte des Urchristentums*. Heidelberg: C. F. Winter, 1928.
Perry, Menahem, and Meir Sternberg. "The King through Ironic Eyes: Biblical Narrative and the Literary Reading Process." *Poetics Today* 7 (1986) 275–322.
Pew Research Center's Religion & Public Life Project. "'Nones' on the Rise." http://www.pewforum.org/2012/10/09/nones-on-the-rise/ October 9, 2012.
Philo Alexandrinus. *Philo: In Ten Volumes (and Two Supplementary Volumes) 3*. Translated by F. H. Colson and G. H. Whitaker. The Loeb Classical Library 247. Cambridge, MA: Harvard University Press, 1960.
Pruyser, Paul W. *The Minister as Diagnostician: Personal Problems in Pastoral Perspective*. Philadelphia: Westminster, 1976.
Pyper, Hugh S. "Modern Gospels of Judas: Canon and Betrayal." *Literature & Theology* 15 (2001) 111–22.
Räisänen, Heikki. *The Rise of Christian Beliefs: The Thought World of Early Christians*. Minneapolis: Fortress, 2010.
Rhoads, David M. "Social Criticism: Crossing Boundaries." In *Mark and Method: New Approaches in Biblical Studies*, edited by Janice Capel Anderson and Stephen D. Moore, 135–61. Minneapolis: Fortress, 1992.
Rhoads, David, and Donald Michie. *Mark as Story: An Introduction to the Narrative of a Gospel*. Philadelphia: Fortress, 1982.
Rhoads, David, and Kari Syreeni, eds. *Characterization in the Gospels: Reconceiving Narrative Criticism*. Journal for the Study of the New Testament Supplement Series 184. Sheffield: Sheffield Academic Press, 1999.
Ricoeur, Paul. "Interpretative Narrative." In *The Book and the Text: The Bible and Literary Theory*, edited by Regina M. Schwartz, 237–57. Cambridge, MA: Basil Blackwell, 1990.
Robinson, James M. "The Gospels as Narrative." In *The Bible and the Narrative Tradition*, edited by Frank McConnell, 97–112. New York: Oxford University Press, 1986.
Rohrer-Walsh, Jennifer. "Coming-of-Age in *The Prince of Egypt*." In *Screening Scripture: Intertextual Connections between Scripture and Film*, edited by George Aichele and Richard Walsh, 77–99. Harrisburg, PA: Trinity Press International, 2002.
Rollins, Wayne G. *Soul and Psyche: The Bible in Psychological Perspective*. Minneapolis: Fortress, 1999.
Sanders, E. P. *Jesus and Judaism*. London: SCM, 1985.
———. *Paul and Palestinian Judaism: A Comparison of Patterns of Religion*. London: SCM, 1977.
Schweitzer, Albert. *The Psychiatric Study of Jesus: Exposition and Criticism*. Translated by Charles R. Joy. Boston: Beacon, 1948.
———. *The Quest of the Historical Jesus: A Critical Study of Its Progress from Reimarus to Wrede*. Translated by W. Montgomery. London: A. & C. Black, 1910.
Smalley, Beryl. *The Study of the Bible in the Middle Ages*. Oxford: Blackwell, 1952.
Stendahl, Krister. *Meanings: The Bible as Document and as Guide*. Philadelphia: Fortress, 1984.
Sternberg, Meir. *The Poetics of Biblical Narrative: Ideological Literature and the Drama of Reading*. Bloomington, IN: Indiana University Press, 1985.
Strauss, David Friedrich. *The Life of Jesus Critically Examined*. Translated by George Eliot. London: G. Allen & Co., 1913.

BIBLIOGRAPHY

Syreeni, Kari. "The Gospel in Paradigms: A Study in the Hermeneutical Space of Luke-Acts." In *Luke-Acts: Scandinavian Perspectives,* edited by Petri Luomanen, 36–57. Publications of the Finnish Exegetical Society 54. Helsinki: The Finnish Exegetical Society, 1991.

Tannehill, Robert C. "The Disciples in Mark: The Function of a Narrative Role." *Journal of Religion* 57 (1977) 386–405.

Theissen, Gerd, and Annette Merz. *The Historical Jesus: A Comprehensive Guide.* Translated by J. Bowden. London: SCM, 1998.

Tolbert, Mary Ann. "Asceticism and Mark's Gospel." In *Asceticism and the New Testament,* edited by Leif E. Vaage and Vincent L. Wimbush, 29–48. London: Routledge, 1999.

Tolkien, J. R. R. *On Fairy-stories.* Expanded edition, with commentary and notes by Verlyn Flieger and Douglas A. Anderson. London: HarperCollins, 2008.

Trebolle Barrera, Julio. *The Jewish Bible and the Christian Bible: An Introduction to the History of the Bible.* Translated by Wilfred G. E. Watson. Leiden: Brill, 1998.

Vermes, Geza. *Jesus the Jew: A Historian's Reading of the Gospels.* 2nd ed. London: SCM, 1983.

Visotzky, Burton L. *Reading the Book: Making the Bible a Timeless Text.* New York: Schocken, 1996.

Walsh, Richard. *Reading the Gospels in the Dark: Portrayals of Jesus in Film.* Harrisburg, PA: Trinity Press International, 2003.

Weiss, Johannes. *Jesus' Proclamation of the Kingdom of God.* Translated and edited by Richard H. Hiers and D. Larrimore Holland. Philadelphia: Fortress, 1971.

Wink, Walter. "Neither Passivity nor Violence: Jesus' Third Way." In *Society of Biblical Literature 1988 Seminar Papers,* edited by David J. Lull, 210–24. SBLSP 27. Atlanta, Scholars Press, 1989.

Winnicott, David W. *Playing and Reality.* London: Tavistock, 1971.

———. "Transitional Objects and Transitional Phenomena." In *Freud and Freudians on Religion: A Reader,* edited by Donald Capps, 211–19. New Haven, CT: Yale University Press, 2001.

Name and Subject Index

Abraham (Abram), 49–51, 57, 60, 88–89
Absalom, 58
Adam, 29, 80–82, 92
allegorical interpretation, 51, 90–93, 96
Alter, Robert, 48, 53
ancient Mediterranean culture, x–xi, 11, 38–42, 47, 93–96
angareia, 95
Aqiba, Rabbi, 51
Arcand, Denys, 43
Auerbach, Erich 49–51, 63–65
Augustine, 51

Bach, Johann Sebastian, 33
Bathsheba, 49, 53–55, 58
Bechtel, Lyn, 80–82
Bible codes; *see* equidistant letter sequences
Bible translations, 6–7, 97
biblical inerrancy, ix–x, 5, 25–27, 30, 96
biblical literalism, ix–x, 6–7, 25–27, 51, 93, 96
Binet-Sanglé, Charles, 67
Blass, Rachel, 103
Brueggeman, Walter, 73

Capps, Donald, 72–74
Caruth, Cathy, 70

characterization in the Bible, xi, 9–10, 11, 18, 41–65, 99–101
The Cloud of Unknowing, 99–100
Conzelmann, Hans, 24
Cool Hand Luke, 43
crisis narratives in the Bible, 71–76

David, xi, 49, 57–59
  and Bathsheba, 53–55, 58
  and Goliath, 58
Deism, 103
de Loosten, George, 67
des Pres, Terrence, 71

Eco, Umberto, 13
Eliab, 58
Eliezer, Abram's servant, 89
Eliezer, Rabbi, 69
end-time expectations, 18–19, 23, 27, 34–35, 37, 62–63, 67–68, 79
Epictetus, 35
equidistant letter sequences, 88–9
Erkkilä, Leena, 12
Esau, 48, 57
Essenes, 37, 85, 88
Eve, 80–2
extremism, x, 2–6, 11, 78
Ezekiel, xi, 68–71

Fairbairn, W. R. D., 77
fantasy

NAME AND SUBJECT INDEX

literary, 29
psychological 10, 11, 30, 65, 66–83, 101–4
fiction
    in the Bible, x, 10, 12–18, 25, 30, 103–4
    Bible in fiction & film 26, 31–3, 41–46, 56
film; *see* fiction
Freud, Sigmund, 43, 67, 77, 102–4
Friedman, Richard Elliot, 59

Gaita, Raimond, 104
Garber, David G., Jr., 69–71
gematria, 88–89
Golden Rule, 36
Good Samaritan, 91–92
The Gospel According to St. Matthew (film by Pier Paolo Pasolini), 32
Grant, Patrick, 5
The Greatest Story Ever Told, 32

Haggai, 61
hanina Ben Dosa, 36–7
Harry Potter, 56
Hillel, Rabbi, 36
Hirsch, William, 67
holy war, 2, 3, 6, 16, 89
Homer, 49–50
Honi the Circle Maker, 36
honor and shame, xi, 18, 38–40, 41, 54, 61, 94–5; *see* ancient Mediterranean culture

idealization, 4–6, 10, 28, 30, 77–83, 96, 103
The Iliad, 49
illusion, religion as, ix, 66–83, 101–4
"immigrant characters", 13
incarnation, xi, 7–9, 22, 28, 74–75, 78–79, 91
Irenaeus of Lyon, 44
Isaac, 49, 57, 60
    binding of, 49–51, 57
Ishmael, Rabbi, 51–52

Jacob, 49, 53, 57, 60
    at Peniel, 57
James, the apostle, 7, 19–20
Jerome, 51
Jesse, 58
Jesus, xi, 7–9, 11, 14, 18–28, 30–49, 51, 59, 61–64, 71–79, 84–86, 88, 90–96, 101, 104
    and the Cynic philosophers, 35
    as a preacher of the end of the world, 23, 27, 34–35, 37, 67–68; *see* end-time expectations
    as healer, 18, 25–27, 31–32, 36–37, 72–73, 76; *see* Jesus, miracles of
    disciples of, 18, 21, 24, 40, 61–63, 71–72, 76–77
    in fiction & film 32–33, 41–46; *see* fiction
    the Jew, 8, 18, 26–27, 35–38, 68
    miracles of, 21, 25–27, 31–32, 36–37, 41, 72–73, 76–78
    parables of, 52, 73
    psychiatric studies of, 67–9
    social radicalism of, 22–4, 27, 37, 76
Jesus of Montreal, 43
Joab, 54
Job, x–xi, 16–18, 30
Johanan ben Zakkai, Rabbi, 36
John
    the apostle, 20
    the evangelist, 21, 23, 25, 38, 46, 61, 84
John the Baptist, 24, 27, 34, 68
St. John Chrysostom, 8
Jonah, x– xi, 14–18, 30
Jonathan, 58
Joseph, 57
Joshua, Rabbi, 61, 63
Judas
    Gospel of, 44–46
    Iscariot, 43–46, 48, 62
Judith, 43
Justin Martyr, 96

Kermode, Frank, 48

NAME AND SUBJECT INDEX

Kierkegaard, Søren, 44
Kimball, Charles, 4
Klein, Melanie, 77, 102
Kohut, Heinz, 103
Kübler-Ross, Elisabeth, 73
Küng, Hans, 103–4

lament,
    God's lament, 74
    psalms of, 73–74
The Last Temptation of Christ (film by Martin Scorsese), 33
Lazarus, 42
literature of survival, 70–71
The Lord of the Rings, 29
Lot, 88
Lucas, George, 29
Luke, the evangelist, 14, 21, 23–25, 41, 45, 84, 94
Luther, Martin, 3

Mahdi, 79
Malachi, 61
Malina, Bruce J., 38
Marcion of Sinope, 90
Mark, the evangelist, 21, 23, 61
Marshall, Katherine, 4
Marx, Karl, 66
Mary Magdalene, 24, 43–44, 48
Matthew, the evangelist, 21, 23, 38, 45, 94
Mendel, Menahem, 98
Michal, 58
Miles, Jack, 9–10, 59
miracles, 21, 25–27, 36–37, 41, 61, 72–73, 75–78, 91
Moses, 8, 20, 21, 37, 53, 56–7, 59–60, 85–88, 93, 97–98, 100
myth in the Bible, 10, 24, 25–30, 59, 80–82, 104

narcissism, 67, 69, 103
narrative gaps, xi, 13, 49–55, 85
"natural religion", 103
Nero, emperor, 89
Newman, Paul, 43

Nietzsche, Friedrich, 46, 104

The Odyssey, 49
Odysseus, 53
oral Torah, 86–7
Origen, 51, 90–91, 96
Otto, Rudolf, 60

Parsons, Terence, 13
Pasolini, Pier Paolo, 32
Paul
    the apostle, x, xi, 7, 18–21, 34, 37, 66, 68, 90, 97, 104
    letters of, 8, 19, 34, 90, 104
Paulus, H. E. G., 26
Perry, Menahem, 53–55
Peter (Cephas)
    the apostle, 19–20, 21, 41, 43, 62, 77
    denial of, 64–5
Pharisees, 19, 31–32, 36–38, 85–86
Philip, the deacon, 84
Philo of Alexandria, 90
Pilate, Pontius, 43–46, 48
The Prince of Egypt, 56
Pruyser, Paul, 105
Pyper, Hugh S., 44–46

Q, the sayings gospel, 23
Qumran community, 88
Quran, 5, 6, 88, 96

religious violence, x, 2–6
"return of religion", 1–2
Rhoads, David, ix–xii, 31
rite of passage, 56, 81
Rohrer-Walsh, Jennifer, 56–57
Rosenberg, Stuart, 43
Rowling, J. K., 56
Rushdie, Salman, 14
Russell, Bertrand, 1

Salome, 43
Samuel, 90
Satan, 16–17, 46, 92
Saul, 58

Schweitzer, Albert, 34–35, 67–69
Scorsese, Martin, 33
scriptural inerrancy; *see* biblical
    inerrancy
secularization, 2, 44–46
self-objects, 103; *see* Kohut, Heinz
Sermon of the Mount, 51, 93–95
Shakespeare, William, 6
Shane, 32
Simon
    of Cyrene, 95
    Peter, *see* Peter
splitting, psychological, 4–5, 10,
    77–79
Star Wars, 29
Stendahl, Krister, x, 30
Sternberg, Meir, 53–55
Stevens, George, 32, 33

Tatian, 96
Teacher of righteousness, 88
Tertullian, 96
therapeutic qualities of biblical texts,
    72–83, 95
Thomas
    the apostle, 24
    Gospel of, 25, 43
Tolkien, J. R. R., 29
transitional phenomena, 102
two natures of Christ, 8–9

Uriah the Hittite, 53–5

van Gennep, Arnold, 56
Visotzky, Burton L., 51, 61, 97–98

Walsh, Richard, 41–43, 47
Weiss, Johannes, 34–35, 67
Wink, Walter, 93–96
Winnicott, Donald W., 4, 77–78,
    102–5
Winnie the Pooh, 13

Zacchaeus, 49
Zechariah, 61

Scripture Index

OLD TESTAMENT

Genesis	29, 57, 59, 89
2:4b–3:24	80–82
14:14	88
22	49–50
50:20–21	57

Exodus	56, 89
14	91
19:9	100
20:2–7	97
20:19	98
22:25–27	95
33:20	60

Leviticus	
19:19	87

Numbers	89

Deuteronomy	
4:15–19	100
6:20–25	60
20:16	89
24:10–13, 17	95
30:11–14	52, 61, 86, 87
34	8
34:10	60

1 Samuel	
16:7	55
17:28	58
17:29	58
17:42–43	58

2 Samuel	
11	53–55
11:11	54
11:27	55

Job	x, xi, 16–18, 30
1:9–11	16–17
38:3	17

Psalms	
91:5–6	74
139:8–12	101

Proverbs	73

Ecclesiastes	
7:29	52

Isaiah	74, 84, 88
2:4	6

Jeremiah	74

Ezekiel	68–71
1:1–28	68
4–5, 12	68
16, 23	69
Hosea	74
Joel	
2:11	34
3:10	7
Amos	
2:6–8	95
Jonah	x, xi, 14–18, 30
1:1–2	14
3:1–3	15
4:10–11	16
Micah	
4:3	6
Haggai	61
Zechariah	61
Malachi	61

NEW TESTAMENT

Matthew	21, 25
3:10	34
4:15	35
5:3	23
5:10–11	35
5:18	51
5:38–42	93–95
5:44–5	35
6:25–34	76
7:7–11	36
7:12	36
7:15–17	100
10:29–31	76
13:52	38
16:22	77
23:23–24	86
26:50	45
27:32	95
Mark	21, 23, 25, 61
1:1	41
2:1–3:6	39
3:1–6	31
4:11	52
10:15	v, 101
10:29–31	22
13:30	34
13:37	63
14:34	34
14:53–54	64
14:66–72	64
15:21	95
16:17	26, 36
Luke	21, 23–25, 41, 45, 90
1:1–4	8, 41
2	14
4:21	88
6:20–25	22, 34
6:29–30	93–95
6:31	36
10:25–37	91–92
12:6–7, 22–31	76
22:35–36	24
24:44	88
John	21, 23, 25, 61
6:35	76
9:22	38
13:26–30	46
14:16	63
15:12	77
Acts of the Apostles	21
2:44–45	24
8:26–40	84

SCRIPTURE INDEX

Romans
3:28	7
7:6	90
10:17	101
12:15	74
13:1	22

1 Corinthians
1:26	20
1:27–28	66
2:1, 4–5	97
12–13	10
13:11	v
13:12	100
15:3–8	19
15:20	18

2 Corinthians
5:16–17	19, 65

Galatians
3:28	9, 20

Philippians
2:6–8	75
2:9–11	75
2:12–13	xi

1 Thessalonians
4:15	34
5:21–22	100

Hebrews
11:1	66

James
2:20	7, 37
2:24	7

2 Peter
1:16	104

1 John
3:2	53

Revelation
	29, 34
13:18	89

www.ingramcontent.com/pod-product-compliance
Lightning Source LLC
Chambersburg PA
CBHW030901170426
43193CB00009BA/706